Changing the Way America Votes
Election Reform, Incrementalism, and Cutting Deals

CHANGING THE WAY AMERICA VOTES
ELECTION REFORM, INCREMENTALISM, AND CUTTING DEALS

Geralyn M. Miller

Studies in Political Science
Volume 20

The Edwin Mellen Press
Lewiston•Queenston•Lampeter

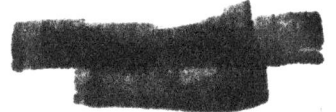

Library of Congress Cataloging-in-Publication Data

Miller, Geralyn M.
 Changing the way America votes : election reform, incrementalism, and cutting deals / Geralyn M. Miller.
  p. cm. -- (Studies in political science ; v. 20)
 Includes bibliographical references and index.
 ISBN 0-7734-6386-0
 1. Voting--United States. 2. Voting-machines--United States. 3. Voter registration--United States. 4. Election law--United States. 5. United States. Help America Vote Act of 2002. I. Title. II. Studies in political science (Lewiston, N.Y.) ; v. 20.

JK1976.M54 2004
324.6'5'0973--dc22

2004048147

This is volume 20 in the continuing series
Studies in Political Science
Volume 20 ISBN 0-7734-6386-0
SPSc Series ISBN 0-7734-7434-X

A CIP catalog record for this book is available from the British Library.

Copyright © 2004 Geralyn M. Miller

All rights reserved. For information contact

 The Edwin Mellen Press   The Edwin Mellen Press
 Box 450   Box 67
 Lewiston, New York   Queenston, Ontario
 USA 14092-0450   CANADA L0S 1L0

The Edwin Mellen Press, Ltd.
Lampeter, Ceredigion, Wales
UNITED KINGDOM SA48 8LT

Printed in the United States of America

*To
Jim and Jamie*

CONTENTS

Preface by Philip R. O'Connor	i
Acknowledgements	iii
Chapter One: How America Votes	1
Safeguarding The Vote	1
The History of Voting in the U.S.	3
Patterns Of Change	10
Conclusion	14
Chapter Two: Identifying The Root Cause(s) Of Voting Problems	17
The Quest For A Villain	17
Research Difficulties	21
Conclusion	31
Chapter Three: The Politics Of Reform	35
A Demand For Change	35
A Collection Of Perspectives	39
Conclusion	55
Chapter Four: Road To Reform	59
Crafting A Compromise	59
A Little For Everyone	75
Conclusion	76
Chapter Five: Cosmetic Fix For A Systemic Problem	79
Prognosis For Success	79
Assigning Blame For Disappointment	89
Conclusion	92
Chapter Six: Democracy And The Future Of Elections In America	93
Policy Change: Evolution/Reform	93
Opportunity Created	99
Appendices	103

Appendix One	104
Appendix Two	115
Appendix Three	122
Selected Bibliography	125
Index	131

PREFACE

It has been reported that Benjamin Franklin upon leaving Independence Hall in Philadelphia on the final day of the 1787 Constitutional Convention was asked, "Well, Doctor, what have we got – a Republic or a Monarchy?". The Founding Father replied, "A Republic, if you can keep it."

Much of human history the past two centuries shows that keeping a republic, once established, is no easy task. The two essential features of the electoral system that underpins the ongoing maintenance of our American republic are the certainty that there will be subsequent elections, thus assuring both winners and losers another day of reckoning and the credibility of the election mechanism. The first however, emerged in the 2000 presidential election as a matter of intense debate and even division in the country.

While the general outlines of the incredibly close 2000 election remain familiar to us all, the precise details have receded into history – if, indeed, they ever were clear. By itself, of course, the difference of just a few hundred votes separating Al Gore and George Bush in Florida would have been little more than a harmless curiosity if either Gore or Bush had won the Electoral College votes of a few more states, making Florida superfluous. Added ingredients, of course, were the anomaly, though perfectly constitutional, of the losing presidential candidate receiving more of the popular vote than did the winner, the escalating battle in state and federal courts and, of course, the cast of easily caricatured characters populating the Florida electoral bureaucracy.

In addition to its role as an unending source of material for the late night TV monologues, Florida assumed the position as Exhibit A for a rapidly developed theory that somehow a particular voting technology – punch cards – was to blame for the problems in Florida that ultimately required resolution by the United States Supreme Court. This theory was at the heart of the Help America Vote Act (HAVA) passed by Congress in 2002. Geralyn Miller's provocative study puts to the test the conventional wisdom that was so quickly formulated during the 24-hour wall-to-wall coverage of the Florida recount and court cases.

Miller's work forces a reconsideration of many of the premises for HAVA and calls into question the expectations for future error-free elections that will free us from the anxiety about falling short of having the credible election mechanisms so essential to public confidence. Her analysis leads us back to an appreciation of the law of unintended consequences and the inescapable implications of the uncertainties associated with the interaction of millions of humans with technology.

Miller does not stop with merely taking on the conventional wisdom that may seem easy prey for a skilled academic researcher. She identifies basic methodological problems in university based studies that seem to single out punch card voting systems as the key culprit in our 2000 election woes.

Importantly, Miller brings a sober minded approach to her task, applying a framework that allows HAVA to be seen in the framework of a long-running, incremental policy process that does not deliver perfection for all time but builds on past progress to produce modest improvement.

While it is unlikely that we will again face the confluence of events that truly tested the constitutional mechanisms handed down to us by the Founders and in successive developments, the reality, we are reminded, is that the very nature of our system tolerates uncertainties and ambiguities as the price for allowing us the flexibility, over time, to adjust our electoral methods to achieve higher levels of essential credibility and confidence.

Philip R. O'Connor, Ph.D.
Member, Illinois State Board of Elections
January 2004

ACKNOWLEDGEMENTS

I would like to begin by thanking Phil O'Connor of the Illinois Board of Elections for taking the time to review the original draft manuscript of this work and for writing the preface. I have greatly appreciated his assistance to me and support of my work over the years.

I would also like to thank my family, especially Jim and Jamie for listening to my endless chatter about this work and for having the good grace to put up with my dedication to the keyboard. Their patience and loyalty was my stability.

I would like to thank several of my colleagues who lent their expertise to this project. Neil Moore listened often and provided good sound practical advice and Mark Myers provided the Frost and Tennyson quotations as well as the means for frequent trips down Illinois' political memory lane. Thank you, also, to Andy Downs and Jim Whitcraft for spending their valuable time in creating the covers that grace this work.

I would like to thank two dedicated public servants. Amy Whitehouse of U.S. Senator Evan Bayh's Office and Mary Honnegger from U.S. Representative Mark Souder's office provided materials from the Congressional Research Service that would have been much more difficult to retrieve without their assistance. Also, thank you Kathy Heller for diligently copyediting this work in your spare time.

Finally, I would like to thank all of those dedicated workers who make our elections happen. They help to make the freedom that we sometimes take for granted a reality.

Chapter One
How America Votes

> *"Most of the change we think we see in life
> is due to truths being in and out of favour."*[i]
> -Robert Frost
> (The Black Cottage)

Safeguarding The Vote

Elections are the fundamental building block of American democracy. Their outcomes serve to chart the course of public policymaking across the country. They should, therefore, operate to provide clear and inviolate evidence of the will of the American people as they exercise their right to a say in decisions that will impact on the direction of their lives as individuals and as a collective people.

Elections in the United States, though, do not always indicate the preferences of the majority of its citizens. Electoral outcomes and public policies can be determined by a minority of voters and are in many elections. Dahl (1956) pointed out long ago that it is not, in fact, the majority that determines electoral outcomes in this country. The majority of citizens do not necessarily turn out to vote. It is a minority of citizens who actively pursue their interests in elections in this country.

The magnitude of this is apparent when one examines the turnout rates in recent presidential elections. In the 1996 presidential election, for instance, only 49.0% of the voting age population in the United States actually turned out to vote. The winner was the preference not of the majority of all of the people in the

United States, but only of the majority of those who turned out to vote. In Election 2000, the turnout rate was only 51.3% for the entire country. An average turnout rate of 55.08% for the 1960 through 2000 presidential elections would seem to indicate that in only rare cases would the majority of Americans actually choose the winner in a presidential election. The winners of electoral contests, then, are determined by preferences of a minority of citizens whose intensity of interest was strong enough to motivate them to vote.

Still, the power of the vote cannot be discounted even if only for its meaning as a symbol of freedom. A breakdown in the medium that delivers the voice of the people, albeit, among only the people who choose to exercise their right to vote, would have the potential to wreak havoc on the American system of self-governance. Although not always an opportunity that Americans avail themselves of, as a people, we want to ensure that if and when we decide to vote, our vote will count.

The presidential election of 2000 stunned people. While voters expected to find out the winner of the election within a few hours of the close of the polls on November 7th, they were surprised to learn that the outcome would take weeks of complex legal and administrative maneuverings to determine. Although not always sophisticated enough to comprehend the import of each legal maneuver, they were, nonetheless, keenly aware that something had to be amiss with the electoral system to have produced this mess of a result. As the days following November 7th turned into weeks, it became clear to many that democracy was not working up to the level of their expectations. Frustration with the situation, and the system, was rampant.

Both broadcast and print media brought the details of the legal maneuverings into the homes of average Americans, providing the equivalent of a crash course on elections that citizens never anticipated having to sit through. Information pertaining to chads, county voting jurisdictions, election officials, absentee ballots, court documents, and so on, became the topic of many conversations from family dinner tables to university research centers. It also became something that appeared, at least at the time, to deeply trouble a good many people across the country. There were plenty of questions floating around, but not a good deal of answers to be found.

Although the consensus of opinion across the country seemed to be that something was terribly wrong with our electoral system, nobody could identify the cause of the problem with any certainty. Election 2000 not only generated a flurry of legal activity toward determining a winner of the election, but sparked a crusade geared at mending the broken system of voting means. The voting reform movement across the United States was given a booster shot, culminating in the passage of what has been deemed a major reform measure: the Help America Vote Act (HAVA) signed into law on October 29, 2002 by President Bush.[ii] The HAVA was an expensive measure with a $3.8 billion appropriation attached to it earmarked for some very specific purposes, all of which were dedicated to the quest to fix things and to make things right again. Many participated in the movement toward reform, but at $3.8 billion, participatory democracy, apparently, does not come cheaply.

The History Of Voting In The U.S.

Viewed in historical terms, reform has been a fundamental part of the American political experience, one that has cropped up frequently in our history. This has been particularly true with regard to the arena of elections. One might ask the question, then, why do we seem to continually quest for voting reform, yet never achieve a lasting system? The answer to that question involves a complex set of circumstances centered around our rational self-interested human nature.

A brief look back at history is helpful to a comprehensive understanding of what we mean by voting reform in the United States. This begins, perhaps, with an understanding of the evolution in the mechanics of voting. Understanding the history of this evolution is an important part of understanding the concept of voting reform in general because it allows us to consider the idea of reform within the broader picture of the events and circumstances that characterize the

American democratic process. The catalyst for voting reform measures that have taken place has been one of two sets of circumstances: technological advancement and elimination of political corruption in elections.

David Orr, Cook County Clerk in Illinois, the county that includes the City of Chicago, was asked how the day's elections had been running on Election Day, November 5, 2002. He responded that things were going fairly well with only a few minor equipment problems that were handled routinely, pointing out that "...if a machine goes down, then people have to vote the old-fashioned way...they put the ballot in the ballot box."[iii]

On that particular election day in 2002, the concept of dropping a ballot into a ballot box was, indeed, considered to be old-fashioned compared to the set of steps involved in voting by use of newer types of voting equipment. A paper ballot system is an antiquated way of voting when compared to, for instance, a Direct Record Electronic (DRE) voting apparatus that tallies votes in a computerized fashion immediately upon the voter casting a vote. It was by no means, though, the first method by which voting occurred.

In American colonial times, ballot boxes that contained paper ballots marked by voters were unheard of. Colonists voted, instead, using a crude means of combining Indian corn and beans. A kernel of Indian corn thrown into a hat in the center of the room in which voting took place signified a vote in favor of an individual's election and a bean signified a vote against his election. Interestingly, there were distinct regulations placed on this voting process by the British Crown to prevent election fraud. A penalty of ten pounds per offense was assessed against any person who was caught throwing more than one kernel of corn or one bean into the hat (Moore, 1884). Obviously, fraud had been an anticipated possibility at that time or sanctions would never have been proposed.

Voting with vegetables, as simplistic and even comical as that appears today, became problematic to the people of colonial times in much the same way as certain types of voting equipment are viewed today. In a documented case of voting irregularity in the Continental Congress of 1776, peas had coincidentally been used instead of the traditional beans in the first recorded vote, while in a subsequent vote on the same measure, a written ballot replaced the irregular one. This raised speculation that the change in legumes may have been partly responsible for shifting the vote to a written paper method for the final outcome of that vote (Moore, 1884). This example illustrates that although the technology was a simple one, it was still capable of being suspect to the people of the time who wanted to safeguard the sanctity of the vote.

Between the mid-17th and early 19th centuries, methods of voting varied between voting by a show of hands and voting by written papers. Some elections were held via the voice vote while others were held through written papers, or as we know them today, paper ballots. Albright (1942) reports that the first state constitutions of the original thirteen colonies detailed written papers as an accepted means of voting. The practice of written voting, though, was not uniformly adhered to for quite some time. Voice vote continued to occur in various elections. The Federal Election Commission (FEC) reports that the State of New York was the first to adopt a statewide system of elections using paper ballots in 1889. Varied means of casting votes has, therefore, a lengthy tradition in the United States.

The FEC identifies five types of voting systems in use across the country.[iv] Paper ballots are still in use in some voting localities, but the actual number of registered voters who reside in those localities amounts to a very small percentage of the overall number of registered voters in the United States. Several other types of voting equipment are much more common in their usage, including mechanical lever machines and punch cards.

The first official use of a mechanical lever-type voting machine dates back to 1892 when it was used for the first time officially, according to the FEC, in the City of Lockport, New York. Mechanical lever machines are large and bulky pieces of equipment that provide a privacy curtain to close behind the voter who votes by pulling down a series of levers that correspond to the individual candidates for office. When the voter has completed voting, he/she then opens the curtain by pulling down another level that locks in a new count of votes within the machine as the voter prepares to exit the booth. These machines caught on quickly because of their efficient means of handling large numbers of votes. They were used in every major city in the United States by 1930 and by over half of the nation's voters by the 1960's. Indeed, the term "voting booth" is derived from this piece of equipment whose original design is attributed to Jan Josef Baranowski of Paris who suggested that adding-machine principles be coupled with voting concepts and that a closet be provided in which the voter can make his/her choice (Albright, 1942). Controversy has always surrounded these machines because of their ability to be tampered with.[v]

The FEC also reports that punch card voting systems have been in use in the United States since they were first adopted for use in Fulton and DeKalb Counties in Georgia in the primary election of 1964. Information provided in subsequent chapters will detail the important role played by the punch card device in leading to recent congressional action that is being touted as the unprecedented voting reform in the United States.

Another piece of equipment currently in use in the United States is the DRE system. This device electronically stores the choices made by the voter into a storage device such as a memory cartridge, diskette or smart-card, immediately upon his/her selection, adding those choices to the existing set of those stored. Approximately 15.0% of the registered voters across the country were eligible to vote using this type of equipment in the 2000 general election (Fife and Miller, 2002). The adequacy of this newest type of voting equipment is a much-debated topic at the present time, as will become clear in Chapter 3, so growth of its usage in the future remains uncertain.

One thing is clear, though, technological advances continue to contribute to the change in the characterization of voting in the United States as it has from the very beginning of the country. Whether these advances have been the result of attempts to curb corruption or simply a by-product of inevitable change in the march toward the future, the point remains that the way in which voting occurs has shifted from one means to another over the course of the nation's history. And, whether changes in voting involve switching from vegetables to paper or from mechanical devices to computerized ones, there are costs involved that must be born by the citizenry at large. Those costs involve decisions that require us to prioritize the expenditure of our scarce resources and, therefore, inevitably lead to differing opinions and, eventually, conflict resulting from opposing ideological perspectives.

American democracy was founded on a set of shared values. As a people, the citizens of the United States of America recognize the need for nurturing those values in an attempt to preserve the ideals spawned by them. Turning ideals into a reality, though, has been fraught with the clash of multiple perspectives.

The lenses through which people view their governing process are as varied as the people themselves. We do not fall neatly into one of two ideological camps: liberal or conservative. Rather, our unique ideologies place us on a continuum that spans a range of infinite possible points between liberalism and conservatism. Those ideologies contribute to our preferences as individuals with regard to public policies. Those who lean in the liberal direction favor a greater degree of governmental protection of the individual right, while conservatives favor a limit on that governmental protection. This includes our view of what we believe to be a sufficient set of rules to govern the voting process for, as Dudley and Gitelson (2002) point out, the rules clearly matter to the outcomes of our electoral contests. While liberals favored more stringent regulation of the voting process and a stronger national governmental presence in a uniformly functioning process, conservatives wanted the states, with their own unique culturally dictated norms and customs, to be free to operate without a great degree of looming national governmental presence.

The degree to which we vacillate between these two perspectives varies by specific topic. Mancur Olson argued that the multiple overlapping group memberships Americans hold define who we are (Olson, 1971). They form the framework on which we build our ideologies. If our preferences shift with the salience of the issue set before us, along with the strength of our attachment to the resources at stake, then the arenas of our daily lives take place within the context of a system that is characterized by a continuous shifting of our individual ideologies.

Those shifts form the basis of American public opinion. They are reflective of the process operating within American society at any given time as groups compete for scarce resources in what Robert Dahl, many years ago, characterized as a pluralistic society, one composed of multiple competing power centers (Dahl, 1961). Decisions are deals arrived at through a series of negotiation and trade-offs between the groups. As these groups compete with one another on specific issues and/or for specific sets of resources, they come away from the process in one of four distinct positions:

1) they have achieved what they consider to be a satisfactory share of the resources;
2) they have achieved what they consider to be an unsatisfactory share of the resources and are poised to seek a larger share;
3) they have failed to achieve a share of the resources, but for a variety of reasons are not willing to immediately seek a larger share; or,
4) they have failed to achieve a share of the resources and are ready to fight all over again.

The specifics of the bargains and deals struck will set up the above conditions and will dictate the ability and duration of the newly enacted measure to exist before a new groundswell for change begins to gel.

Over the course of the past several decades, we have witnessed a proliferation of groups in both the federal (Cigler and Loomis, 2002; Schlozman, Lehman and Tierney, 1986; Walker, 1983 and 1991) and state (Rosenthal, 1993) arenas. This posits the public affairs arena as inherently one of conflict, resplendent with bargaining and deal-making among the groups, and the elected officials as decision-makers. Each group vies for what it perceives to be its rightful share of a limited set of resources. Likewise, each elected official struggles, personally, in deciding how to allocate those resources, and politically in working toward making the choice they have made to become a policy reality.

The nature of our federal system of governance contributes toward making policy formulation and implementation a difficult matter. Although each state administers voting within its own borders, over the past four decades the federal government, through such measures as the Voting Rights Act, the Motor Voter Act, and, most recently, the HAVA, has increasingly intruded on these domains, making it difficult for the states to uniquely administer the process of elections.

The states are hubs of electoral activity characterized by differences in the administration of elections. Voting requirements, usage of equipment, primary election systems, and so on all vary. Above all else, the people differ in their customs, habits, socioeconomic resources, and preferences.

The states contribute, therefore, uniquely to the election of federal officeholders. Perhaps, this collection of individual uniquely bred contributions is reflective of the spirit of democracy that our founding fathers deliberately incorporated into the governing system through the design of the American electoral system as it is outlined in the United States Constitution supported by the Tenth Amendment.

As a result, there is a dynamic set of conditions in the American political arena generated over each decision made within the confines of the American democratic institutions. There are no exceptions since as long as there is scarcity of resources, there will always be friction present. No single decision can satisfy all of the groups competing for a limited set of resources. When you have winners, you usually have losers. As I detailed in an earlier work, there exists a pendulum swing in America with regard to public opinion and ideology that results in a perpetual resculpting of our public policies that serve to align those policies with what appears to be the truth at any given point in time.[vi] Since our foundations are built on documents that reflect general principles rather than fixed rules, the crafting and implementation of those policies are inherently open to interpretation in an ongoing process.

Patterns Of Change

Inherent within this dynamic set of conditions in the environment of American public opinion is a temporal dimension that produces changes in the levels and characterization of that ongoing process described in the previous paragraph. Throughout that process, our knowledge changes. What we think we know becomes obsolete, replaced by the next level of knowledge in a constant march toward the future.

Change is an inevitable, if elusive, part of our lives, the importance of which cannot be overstated. Leon Martel (1986) pointed out that understanding change is a key to being able to successfully manage our affairs and that this understanding begins with a recognition of the difference between cyclical and structural change. Cyclical change is change that occurs in the operation of some entity or process that can be identified through its patterns over time. Alteration of conditions caused by cyclical change is temporary. Structural change, on the other hand, creates a permanent alteration of the character and composition of the phenomena. It can occur rapidly or it can occur slowly over a lengthy period of time, but once it occurs, conditions are irrevocably altered.

By its very nature, voting reform is about change. When we seek to reform our electoral process, we seek to improve on it. Ideally, we seek a permanent improvement, but as Martel demonstrated, improvement to a process usually involves cyclical change because it is difficult to fundamentally or structurally alter a process since process is dependent upon the existing knowledge of the time period in which it occurs.

The nature of specific changes determines the agenda for future action. If the electoral process is fundamentally altered, the problems that catalyzed the change cease to exist. Alternatively, if the electoral process is temporarily, or cyclically, altered, the problems will continue to crop up in the future at varying points in the process.

On the one hand, voting reform involves cyclical change. At various stages throughout our history, the voting equipment that we use and the rules by which we vote have been altered. In 1897, for instance, just a little over 100 years ago, the State of California established a commission to investigate current voting equipment to assess its accuracy and efficiency in terms of registering the will of the voters (Albright, 1942). Other states engaged in similar types of reform measures that allowed for the adoption of newer types of voting equipment and their placement in voting jurisdictions. Closely tied to accuracy and efficiency, fears of voting fraud prompted investigations into and changes of voting equipment. Historian Loomis Mayfield (1993) provides us with an in-depth account of one such type of change in the City of Pittsburgh in the early twentieth century in a case study of election reform in that city that underscores the importance of temporal considerations in conceptualizing voting reform as well as understanding that public perception of the existence of vote fraud is equally capable of producing reform movements as is the reality of vote fraud. He notes in his Pittsburgh case study that although the reform movement was advanced on the notion of vote fraud, retrospective analysis does not provide much evidence of the occurrence of actual vote fraud. Now, these many years later, we have engaged in a similar investigation and reform measure, this time nationwide in its scope and based in large measure on allegations of inaccuracies and inefficiency of the voting equipment in use, as well as in the disparate treatment of voters by election administrators.

On the other hand, voting reform involves structural change, as well. Once reform measures are instituted, our system of voting is fundamentally altered. Voting with corn and beans will, probably, never be used again and lever machines will become antiques, novelties at county fairs and in museums. Our expectations as voters change once we experience something new and there is never a return to what was.

Understanding the concept of change is fundamental to successful public policymaking. The knowledge we hold today is limited in comparison to what we will know tomorrow. Yet, scholars repeatedly fail to take this into consideration when analyzing present-day societal problems. In a 1927 article that appeared in the prestigious *American Political Science Review* with regard to innovation and diffusion of mechanical voting apparatus policy, political scientist T. David Zukerman (1927) wrote:

> In the light of its recent history, it will be difficult to raise any further questions regarding the mechanical efficiency of the voting machine and the ability of voters to use it. The only improvements of any importance which may be looked for in the future are refinements intended to convince the individual voter that his vote is being registered in accordance with his desires...[vii]

Clearly, technological advance was not anticipated in this comment. Yet, it is curiously prophetic in its insight into the inability of present-day technology to satisfy future concerns. The reform movement that culminated in the passage of the HAVA was, in large measure, catalyzed by the fears of certain groups of voters that their individual votes were not being recognized.

Voting reform is no different in its process from any other public policy in the making. Rather, it differs from ordinary policy evolution only in its strategic intent. Reform is a messy business as is any policymaking process. As Charles Lindblom (1959) argued, much public policy comes about by "muddling through" the mess rather than by any comprehensive logical program. In the majority of cases in which public policies come to be created, they do so through a series of incremental steps. They are developed not through a rational process that identifies the workable solutions from an exhaustive list of every possible alternative, but rather through a list of constrained alternatives obtained from a compilation of the most readily available and feasible set of policy alternatives. They are refined in a slow steady manner through the implementation and evaluation stages of the policy in practice. American public policymaking is, in the main, a very disorderly process accomplished by placing one foot in front of the other and learning with each step. With several notable exceptions, it is incremental to its core.

Perhaps, the creation of the United States Constitution exemplifies this better than any other case. Americans like to romanticize the history of the Constitution, portraying the framers as men of genius who came to develop a document like none other, one that has sustained the tests of time. The truth of the matter is that the constitutional document has had to be amended numerous times in order to withstand those tests. The original document was the result of a set of deals struck among the mortal men we refer to reverently as our Founding Fathers. It was a product of intense compromise and negotiation brought about by what, today, we would call lobbying and public relations campaigns evidenced by the Federalist Papers and the Great Compromise, for instance. It is also a product that continues to evolve as we seek to incorporate the changes that take place into our system of self-governance. If that history is any indication, there are likely to be additional amendments yet to come.

Mortin Grodzins (1966) has likened the federal structure of American government to that of a layer cake where the layers represent the various levels of government in the American governmental system. But a layer cake is a static object, which once baked, becomes a solidified form that is incapable of reforming except through its destruction. Our system is much more like the marble fudge one can find being made in the many tourist attractions across America. The marbling changes with each sweep of the spatula until it solidifies into a specific pattern. Unlike a cake, though, fudge is malleable. It can be formed and reformed into differing patterns simply by adjusting the pressure and temperature. So, too, the constant pressure exerted by the continuous cycle of change that produces a shifting public opinion and interest group activity in America serves to alter the pattern of our system as reflected in the specific contours of the public policies that we craft. Sometimes it changes through the normal course of daily activities, sometimes through a strategic initiative.

The propensity to romanticize is apparent in our understanding of the concept of reform also. Reform, simply defined, is an alteration brought about by change of form and is expected to have positive outcomes. As discussed above, change comes both cyclically and structurally, but in terms of public policy, there seems to be a tacit assumption of permanency when we seek to reform. This work demonstrates that we do not have a realistic impression of voting reform as a concept since there is a fundamental belief that our policies, while incrementally designed within the constraints discussed above, are permanent fixes to the problems that plague us. Permanent reform, we never seem to understand, is only a dream, a nirvana.

Conclusion

In sum, this work demonstrates that voting reform, a change to our most basic process of participatory democracy in the United States, like anything else is one constrained temporally and spatially by what E. E. Schattschneider (1975) referred to many years ago as pressure politics. The process of voting in the United States is one characterized by continual change dictated by changing technology and interest group activity.

Recent events in voting reform in America are characterized by methodological difficulties rooted in cultural, ideological, and paradigmatic considerations. Pressure politics resulted in forcing us into a voting policy that may very well have some unintended consequences, ones that could detract from the health of the democratic process.

Chapter 2 will engage in the identification of a few of the difficulties that have caused the nature of the voting problem to remain elusive. Exploration of those problems will demonstrate that the recent reform measure was driven by a panicked reaction to bits and pieces of knowledge rather than by a logical advance toward problem resolution.

Chapter 3 will provide an overview of the opinions presented and work undertaken by a variety of players in the public process in their attempt to clearly define the problem as they work toward arriving at a solution. Players in the voting reform arena including academics, politicians and political parties, lawyers, minority groups, administrators, and the citizenry at large are at odds with each other in their struggle to identify both the complexities of the problem and an adequate solution to it, as they struggle for positioning in the battle to implement equal protection in voting.

In Chapter 4, I will argue that several factors work against systemic voting reform. Although we now have an existing reform measure that is hailed as a bipartisan solution to recent voting problems, the outcome of this measure is far from certain. Presented to the American people as sweeping reform, this measure is one developed as a negotiated compromise between interested groups.

Chapter 5 will engage in a discussion of the inadequacies of the reform measure in the world of practical electoral activity. The myth of achieving a perfect electoral system through the current vision of voting reform will be discussed.

Finally, Chapter 6 concludes the book with a discussion of the implications of this research and will seek to answer the question of what the impact from voting reform will be on the democratic process in America. This is the question that all players should be addressing in their quest to retool the mechanism through which America carries out its self-governing system.

Notes

[i] Frost, Robert. 1915. *North of Boston*. New York, NY: Henry Holt and Company.
[ii] Help American Vote Act of 2002. Pub. L. 107-252, Oct. 29, 2002. 116 Stat. 1666.
[iii] David Orr interviewed on WBBM radio in Chicago on November 5, 2002.
[iv] The five types of voting equipment in use in the U.S. as identified by the FEC are: paper ballot, mechanical lever machine, punch card, optical scan, and DRE.
[v] For a full discussion of this see "A Modern Democracy That Can't Count Votes." Editorial, *Los Angeles Times*, December 11, 2000.
[vi] This reference to a pendulum swing in public opinion and ideology is contained in the last chapter of Fife, Brian and Geralyn M. Miller. 2002. *Political Culture in the United States*. Westport, CT: Greenwood Publishing, but was written solely by Miller.
[vii] Zukerman, T. David. 1927. "The Voting Machine Extends Its Territory." *American Political Science Review*. 21 (3)603-610, p. 609.

Chapter Two

The Elusive Root Cause(s) of America's Voting Problems

> *"He who has not first laid his foundations may be able with great ability to lay them afterwards, but they will be laid with trouble to the architect and danger to the building."*
> -Machiavelli
> (The Prince)

The Quest For A Villain

Conventional wisdom among scholars, media commentators, the working press and politicians in the United States today holds that the voting technology used in U.S. elections played an important role in Election 2000 by virtue of the high rate of voting error. Specifically, the punch card system of voting seems to be targeted as the villain.

Media portrayals of dangling and pregnant chads being debated over by countless election officials in the days and weeks following the presidential election gave the distinct impression to readers and viewers that this system was, indeed, in need of attention. At the same time, it was surprising to the many voters who were accustomed to using a different type of voting equipment from that of punch cards. Since there are five distinct types of voting systems employed across the country, many folks were unaware that punch card equipment even existed, let alone that it could be capable of producing such a severe set of problems.

Information available to citizens since Election 2000 has helped to fuel distrust of this particular type of voting equipment. In a recent op-ed piece that appeared in the *Chicago Tribune*, the Legal Director of the American Civil Liberties Union (ACLU) of Illinois claimed, "virtually all other voting systems perform better than punch cards."[i] This statement that singles out punch cards as particularly pernicious in the set of troubles surrounding Election 2000 was made matter-of-factly, as though it were common factual knowledge.

Yet, is it a factual reality that punch card systems were to blame for unexpectedly high rates of voting error in Election 2000 or any other election, for that matter? Are punch card systems truly more error-prone than the four other types of voting systems currently used in the United States? Or, was conventional wisdom the product of surface looks at complex issues coupled with intense ideological perspective and an inability to understand the importance of identifying the origins of the information we encounter? An in-depth review of the factual information available on this subject is in order for an answer to this question.

A search for an explanation of the voting problems in the wake of Election 2000 quickly turned to the voting equipment. Political science scholars from Caltech and MIT Universities, for example, joined together in a study funded by the Carnegie Foundation that sought to explain the reason(s) for the problems of Election 2000 through examination of the voting equipment. Consider that in their report, they indicated the following conclusion:

> The central finding of this investigation is that manually counted paper ballots have the lowest average incidence of spoiled, uncounted, and unmarked ballots, followed closely by lever machines and optically scanned ballots. Punch card methods and systems using direct recording electronic devices (DREs) had significantly higher average rates of spoiled, uncounted, and unmarked ballots than any of the other systems.[ii]

The data examined by these researchers led them to conclude that there were, indeed, differences among the various types of voting equipment with regard to their measure of voting error, but that it was two distinct types of equipment that appeared to present higher error rates.

Comments made in the *Chicago Tribune* op-ed piece by the Legal Director of the ACLU, therefore, are in conflict with the findings of these researchers, since the latter identify both DRE devices and punch cards as having

19

significantly high rates of error. Yet, the ACLU indicated that only one type of equipment was problematic and it was disseminated as though it was an undisputed fact. The ACLU is a well-established organization that has grown in its reputation for guarding liberty and preserving individual rights from its small group of founding anti-war activist members in 1920 to its nearly 300,000 members and supporters today. It is currently, and has been throughout its history, active in a variety of state and national civil rights campaigns that make its acronym a household term. Undoubtedly, many who read the piece in the *Chicago Tribune* did take it as fact, particularly those who view the ACLU as a credible source of information.

The Caltech/MIT study was one of the first efforts put forth to identify the cause of the voting problems and, as such, should be viewed cautiously until further testing is done to validate it. Early research is often methodologically challenged and, subsequently, by later research. Careful review of the methods used in the Caltech/MIT study would seem to indicate the need for additional research. At any rate, placing total reliance on the findings from that study is premature at this point.

Specifically, Caltech/MIT researchers made a basic methodological error when they chose to analyze county election data. The county is normally the jurisdiction responsible for the administration of elections throughout the various states, but there are exceptions. In Maine, the townships and/or municipalities are responsible for elections. Results of analysis on counties cannot be generalized to these. Furthermore, results of this study were garnered from analysis of a set of data generated from counties in multiple states when the administration of elections is a state activity, not a federal one. A better way to utilize the data is to treat them as individual case studies so that statistical techniques can be tailored to the unique characteristics of the data as they exist within the individual states. In this way, the factors influencing voting error can be isolated and, perhaps, more easily detected. In other words, combining the data from multiple states may invalidate the conclusions drawn from results of the study.

It is possible that when the data are combined, the true effects of any intrastate influences on voting error, such as the interaction of voting technology and specific groups of voters due to socioeconomic factors, particularly educational levels, may be obscured. It is inconceivable that while political scientists acknowledge the link between voting behavior and socioeconomic conditions, they find it so difficult to entertain the idea that, perhaps, those influences may impact on the mechanics of voting, as well, or that actually implementing elections may be more difficult in some areas than in others. To date, scant attention has been paid by the scholarly community to the practical considerations involved in administering elections and that varying socioeconomic conditions may create difficulties, in some areas, to providing equal protection of the vote of all persons in those other areas. Simply concluding that the equipment is at fault is a premature conclusion to draw.

There are those who have cautioned against an over-reliance on the initial Caltech/MIT study:

> Based upon our own analysis of data for the 2000 election and our concerns with these problems, we advise against the rush to judgment of the Caltech/MIT report...much more testing of the available systems is needed before making any final judgments about the suitability of one system over another.[iii]

The conventional wisdom failed to take this into consideration because the nature of the statistics is too sophisticated for most audience members to comprehend. Also, since the study sample represented an impressive amount of data coupled with the fact that researchers came from two of America's most prestigious institutions of higher learning, those angry with the results of Election 2000 eagerly accepted the news that punch card voting technology was more error-prone than many of the other types of equipment in use as proof positive that the technology was partly to blame. What is particularly troubling is that this news was so eagerly accepted by many who should have viewed these study results as a first step in solving a very complex puzzle, but instead, readily hailed those findings as a key to fixing the problem. The average person in society does not have adequate training to be able to interpret statistical findings. In the absence of appropriate statistical training, it is understandable that the results indicated by the Caltech/MIT researchers appeared to be acceptable.

Research Difficulties

One might ask, then, why these researchers modeled their data set as they did when there might be better ways of modeling it. Perhaps, the answer to that question lies in the difficulties inherent in the collection of state-level voting data. Although all research takes place, to a degree, within a set of constraints, research on voting behavior and the administration of voting systems within the individual states is particularly problematic. Each state administers its elections in a unique manner, one that is consistent with the culture of the state. In fact, Fife and Miller (2002) found that the political culture of a state is an important determinant of the choice of voting equipment employed within the state, so the administration of elections within the states is directly tied to the unique culture of the state (Fife and Miller, 2002). Several researchers have attempted to define and categorize the political culture of the states for purposes of determining its impact on various public policy innovations/diffusions and electoral outcomes but no scheme has been devised, as yet, which appears to satisfy all of the researchers interested in this variable (Elazar, 1994; Jewell, 2001). However, although there has been a good deal of controversy as to how to define and/or classify the unique political cultures that exist across the states, there is a general consensus of opinion as to the fact that the cultures do vary. As a result, the particulars of the administration of those systems differ widely across the states, as well.

For instance, most states require counties to supply election vote data to a central state repository such as an elections division in a secretary of state's office or a separate state election board. Again, the institutional arrangement is dependant upon the particular state. The specific data collected varies also. Some of the states require a good deal of detail and specificity in the data that they collect while others collect a few basic descriptive figures from the local units of government.

The administrative structure in each individual state often characterizes the nature of the data collection, retention, and availability within that state. States that tend to have strong centralized electoral warehousing, and those with large shares of resources allotted to those functions, are most likely better able to support those activities than are states that have a more decentralized warehousing perspective and that leave those functions up to the individual local election authorities at the county or municipal level.

An example of this can be found in looking at the differences in the 2000 annual operating budgets for election-related operations in several states. The figures encountered in a random sample of fifteen states demonstrate that a good deal of variation exists in the amounts of resources available for the purpose of overseeing elections in these states. Figures ranged from a low of $20,532 in Nevada where the 2000 voter registration comprised 874,304 voters to a high in Florida of $23,878,752 with a registration of 8,752,717. This translates to roughly $.02 for every voter in Nevada, as opposed to $2.73 in Florida.[iv] Obviously, the potential data collection and warehousing capacity of a state like Nevada will be nowhere near that of a state like Florida. Furthermore, what the election authorities within the individual states deem as important information will also vary. The result is a mixed bag of data collected and stored across the states. For researchers this translates into extreme difficulties in accessing complete sets of usable data from the full set of states and studies that are limited in both validity and generalizability.

Several examples help to clarify this point. Although there was a central repository at the state level in Pennsylvania in 2000 for housing county-level data, while that agency collected vote totals by office, it did not require counties to provide the actual number of ballots cast in given elections. In the case of Texas at that time, and as of this writing, the actual number of ballots cast was only an approximation assigned by state authorities. The true number was not collected from the counties. Obviously, in these two states, both of which are crucially important in terms of Electoral College votes, trained social scientists would not be able to rely on the state to provide accurate data. They would be forced to contact each county independently, a process that could be time consuming and monetarily costly given that there are over three hundred counties in those two states combined. Researchers operate within a set of constrained resources in the work they do. They usually do not have the luxury of analyzing a perfect data set. Sometimes, even finding a sample that approximates a fairly representative one is difficult. Yet, the point remains that science requires that researchers continue to pursue problems until they have exhausted all possible alternatives in their quest to advance knowledge.

The nature and comprehensiveness of a state's data collection will impact on researchers' ability to adequately measure concepts. This appears to have been the case with the Caltech/MIT residual voting error study since, in fact, these two particular states, Pennsylvania and Texas, were among a group of seventeen states noticeably absent from the data set used by them. Researchers mention within the study that these seventeen states were omitted because the data they were able to obtain from the states were insufficient to calculate residual vote. They were fully aware of this problem. A study conducted by the U.S. Congressional Judiciary Committee (2001) indicated that nineteen secretaries of state indicated that their states kept no records on the numbers of uncounted ballots, when questioned about voting error in Election 2000. The problem of assessing voting error, given this large gap across the country in accurate records, posed a major problem for researchers, political practitioners, interest groups, news media, and others who attempted to get a handle on this phenomenon.

Another problem facing researchers with regard to the question of voting error and technology is the manner in which the residual vote is calculated. At the present time, the residual vote is commonly measured as the difference between ballots cast and votes garnered in particular races. For example, if there were 550 ballots cast in a voting jurisdiction, 500 votes cast for U.S. President, and 450 votes cast for U.S. Senator, then the residual votes for those offices would be 50 and 100, respectively. This assumes that there is no purposive or intentional activity on the part of voters to omit voting for either of those offices. Obviously, some people will, for a variety of reasons, decide not to vote for specific offices. Unfortunately, in the absence of other data, this is the best measure that is available to approximate this figure. Eventually, and in light of the recent recognition by administrators of the importance of keeping adequate statistical records, researchers will seek out and find a better measure of what constitutes a residual vote. At the present time, though, this is all that is available to work with.

The subjectivity inherent in deciding what constitutes a spoiled ballot, was taken into consideration in the *Bush v. Gore* decision by the Supreme Court in stating:

> while the state's basic command for the count of legally cast votes – to consider the intent of the voter – is unobjectionable as an abstract proposition and a starting principle, the formulation of uniform rules to determine a voter's intent is practicable and necessary in this instance, where the question is not whether to believe a witness, but how to interpret the marks or holes or scratches on an inanimate ballot card, a piece of cardboard or paper, which might not have registered as a vote during the machine count; 2) the want of those rules has led to the unequal evaluation of ballots.[v]

As long as counting votes is left up to a system designed by humans, there will be problems. Humans are not perfect; they are incapable of designing perfect systems.

The degree to which voters were disenfranchised by the voting problems seems as though it might vary along socio-economic lines, but there are conflicting bits of evidence as to the reality of this. The U.S. Commission on Civil Rights found in its study of the Florida 2000 voting situation that:

> Poor counties, particularly those with large minority populations, were more likely to possess voting systems with higher spoilage

rates than the more affluent counties with significant white populations.[vi]

On the other hand, researchers Stephen Knack and Martha Kropf (2002) found that there was no basis for this allegation in their study of the placement of voting equipment systems across the country. Punch card systems were just as likely to be found among the voting jurisdictions in which concentrated numbers of white voters were located as those in which concentrated numbers of minority group voters were in the counties that they studied across the country. Again, what is the truth here? Are these pieces of equipment disproportionately placed among the lower socioeconomic voting populations or is this a myth? We simply don't have enough information to make an adequate assessment of this issue at this point.

At the Institute of Government and Public Affairs at the University of Illinois at Champaign-Urbana, researchers found that certain types of optical scan voting equipment appeared to be even more problematic than punch card equipment in a study that they conducted using data solely from the State of Illinois.[vii] Results of this study, conducted using data from Illinois only, seems to refute the contention by the Caltech/MIT researchers. Of course, several possibilities exist that could explain this result.

First, it is possible that Illinois is an outlier and not representative of the average state. Concentrated minority populations throughout the state, geographical size of the state, a sectional divide between northern and southern portions of the state, and/or an urban-rural divide, could all possibly contribute to making this case an exception to the rule.

Second, it is possible that when introduced into a larger set of data, the true nature of the problem is obscured. On the other hand, it is also possible that when data are examined within individual states and not across states, the results will be different since the administration of voting occurs within and not across states. There is a void with respect to studies that test for the effects of equipment on an intrastate basis only. Therefore, much more work needs to be done before we can claim an understanding of the link between voting equipment and residual vote.

Conventional wisdom that attributes voting error to voting technology also acknowledges the inadequacies of maintaining voter registration systems across the states as a major cause of electoral deficiencies in this country. Getting rid of punch card systems, alone, will not alleviate all of the problems associated with voting. A host of articles and op-ed pieces appeared in the newspapers across America in the weeks following Election Day 2000, raising concerns about flaws and difficulties associated with maintenance of voter registration lists across the states and prompting discussion about the effectiveness of certain provisions of the National Voter Registration Act (NVRA) of 1993 with regard to maintenance of voter registration lists. Of particular focus were provisions in the NVRA that prevented states from removing voters simply for failure to vote. States were required under the NVRA to wait for a period involving two federal election cycles before removing individuals who had failed to vote in those elections. Practically, this provision created a major problem for maintaining accurate voter registration lists since voters are not required to notify election authorities if they move to another jurisdiction or out of state.

Many anecdotal accounts in those news articles appear to attest to the problems associated with inadequately maintained voter registration lists in the State of Florida during that time period. An article that appeared in the *Miami Herald* on December 7, 2000 stated there were claims by African-American groups that many people had been "turned away from the polls because their names had disappeared from voter registration lists."[viii] That number, ultimately, proved to be quite small. Logically, though, if people are not allowed to vote even though they have registered to do so, the voter turnout figures collected by election authorities will be inaccurate. While it appears that voter turnout is quite low in our elections, the figures may be inflated due to inaccuracies such as this.

Although there is little evidence to suggest that the purge provisions of the NVRA have had any major effect on increasing voter participation levels across the states, our knowledge of problems relating to voter registration lists and their possible link to voting disenfranchisement are a much understudied phenomenon by the scholarly community and could benefit, greatly, from sound empirical studies into the existence and nature of problems of this sort (Knack, 1995; Rhine, 1996). Most of the existing studies use either the voting age population, which disregards turnout and disenfranchisement altogether, or they rely on existing voter turnout statistics that may be generated from inadequately purged lists. In either case, a more accurate assessment of voter registration and its role, if any, in association with electoral voting problems, is crucial to an in-depth understanding of the incidence and nature of voting error and voting difficulties.

Concern has been raised over other issues related to potential voter disenfranchisement in elections, also. Media reports following Election 2000 were filled with anecdotal accounts of members of minority groups being turned away from the polls because of failure to produce an acceptable piece of identification with a photo ID such as a valid driver's license. While the media has featured this topic enough to place it onto the agenda set before the American public, and there has been significant discussion of it, there appears to be little empirical support for the validity of these claims. Voter registration requirements vary by state and some states do require proof of registration via photo identification. Yet, there appears to be little evidence to attest to any disparate treatment along racial lines in the enforcement of this regulation. The scholarly community has had little interest in this topic and there does not appear to be any sound evidence provided for these claims, as yet, that has conclusively been brought forth in any of the lawsuits filed by minority groups against election authorities in the states that would validate the claims. At least for the present, they appear to be allegations that have not been substantiated beyond the anecdotal level.

Attempting to determine the root cause of voting error through empirical research is inherently a difficult task, particularly if one subscribes to the logical positivist tradition of science, a school of philosophy that takes verification of knowledge as essential to science. It is possible to scientifically test only knowledge that is capable of being experienced. Karl Popper (1992/1959), one of the great modern day philosophers argued that since reality is assessed only through the experience of our senses, it is not possible to prove causation in the social sciences. At best, what we infer as the cause of a problem is only a statistically probable estimate, forever subject to the condition of potential falsification. Our truths are tentative ones, always vulnerable, cemented only by corroboration, and in some circumstances, replaced by new vision when falsified in other circumstances. Even under an ideal set of data collection conditions, which we do not have, the knowledge that we gain is not proven knowledge, but only an interpretation of observation that has yet to be disproven. As Popper argued, we can never prove our theories, we can only disprove them. This is a concept overlooked, for the most part, in the public policymaking process.

One big problem in public policymaking is that since we never really know if we have identified the root cause of a social problem, given that we cannot prove our findings, we cannot be certain that measures designed to countermand the problem, our chosen solutions, will work or will not create even bigger problems. As a result, we often face unintended consequences from our policy decisions. In these instances, we set about creating policies that will alleviate problems based on what we believe to be identified causes of those problems only to find that the solutions cause even worse problems for us. It is in society's best interests, therefore, to engage in a good deal of exploration into the root causes of the problems that we encounter in the public domain before we set about attempting to solve them. In view of the possibility of future unintended consequences resulting from a failure to properly identify a true cause, incremental public policymaking is far more efficient in the long run than comprehensive overhaul would be. It is much easier to retract small steps and rechart the course toward solution than it is to return from a solution that involves a series or process of complex circumstances. We will return to a more in-depth discussion of this later in this work in the material contained in Chapters 4 and 6. For now, it is important to note only that if one believes Popper was on the right track, then as he pointed out, every exploration of causation will be problematic because it is a quest for one single truth in an arena in which there are no law-like general conditions because of the varied nature of human beings.

Another source of difficulty from a methodological standpoint is the lens with which we encounter the voting phenomenon. Quite possibly, that lens may impact on the way in which we study the problem. For the most part, those interested in studying voting outcomes are members of the political science community. In attempting to identify problems of voting error, though, it is not simply the outcomes that matter. As was evident in the media portrayals of problems in Election 2000, the administration of the voting systems can impact on the outcome. It is necessary, therefore, to study not just the outcomes, but the administration of the elections and the outcomes simultaneously. As Woodrow Wilson pointed out in 1887, in what many attribute to be the beginning of the study of public administration, there is a decisive difference between the study of politics and the study of government.[ix] While politics is a game of "who gets what, when, where, and how,"[x] government is about carrying out the will of the winners of that game moderated by the knowledge that the losers are watching. Nowhere is this more apparent than in the road to placing election reform in its proper perspective.

The manner in which knowledge is acquired fundamentally impacts on the way in which we interpret events around us. There are two distinct ways in which we acquire the knowledge we hold. We know things through our own experiences and we know those things that we are told (Babbie, 2001). The things that we experience are grounded in our cognition. We accept them because our senses absorb them. On the other hand, things that we have been told constitute our agreement reality, as is often the case with prevailing conventional wisdom. We accept these pieces of knowledge when they come to us through what we perceive to be credible or authoritative sources (Graber, 1993). Information that we receive from individuals who we trust and/or respect will be met with our acceptance. Agreement reality need not be based on factual knowledge, then, to be believable.

It need only be delivered by what each individual uniquely perceives to be a credible source.

The scientific quest for knowledge combines aspects of both experiential and agreement learning. The scientific method demands a rigorous adherence to the methods dictated by the norms and conventions upon which the particular discipline that encompasses the subject matter dictates. Kuhn (1996) points out how normal science occurs within the long-established paradigms that serve as the foundation and/or testing ground for the advancement of knowledge. These paradigms serve to provide a culturally shared perspective among researchers who focus on similar phenomena and/or problems. They provide a means for examining these concerns within the community in order to provide a forum in which theories generated from examination of the problems are validated by others with a shared perspective and expertise. That forum normally occurs in scientific conference panel meetings and refereed scholarly journals.

Much of the policymaking that takes place in the American public affairs arena, on the other hand, is based on agreement reality only. Commonly, the knowledge that policies are generated from is not knowledge that has been validated by normal science. In a rush to accommodate the demands of the citizenry, demands that can make or break political careers, scientific inquiry is left behind. Policies are designed and implemented from knowledge based on mere conjecture. As will become clear in the remainder of this book, recent election reform measures are based largely on agreement reality. As a result, the probability for incidence of unintended consequences is higher than it might be if the reform measures were subjected to the rigors of heuristic examination prior to their adoption.

Finally, a discussion of inherent difficulties of researching social phenomena would be incomplete without at least a mention of the role of ideology. Many years ago, Frank Sorauf (1957) argued that the American public interest was a concept difficult to define and one that should not be dictated by the community of political scientists. He argued that the essence of knowledge distilled through the paradigmatic funnel of normal science may yield a view of what is best for the American public that is vastly different from the expectations of the majority. The elite scientific perspective may not point toward a road that will take the American people where they want to go in their endless quest for self-government. It is, therefore, imperative that members of the political science community not attempt to dictate parameters of the "public interest."

This may be easier advised, though, than accomplished in practice. American political scientists are, after all, wrapped up in the very phenomenon that they seek to explain. As researchers, we cannot separate our civic selves from our scientific selves. We are invested in our research by the nature of our lives as American citizens. The stake that we hold in defining the problem of voting error clouds our judgement in identifying potential causes of the problem. The very questions that we ask are predicated on the beliefs and attitudes that we hold, not only as researchers, but also as citizens. This is where the channels of normal science will have their most important impact. They will serve to act as a check on the limitations that we have as individuals and researchers who hold distinct ideologies that are separate from the shared perspectives that underlie our paradigms and that may serve to bias the direction of our research.

In the end, we can only make suggestions to decision-makers who chart the future of our policies. Ultimately, we are simply one group, albeit, a divided one at times, of the many groups interacting in the pluralistic process of policymaking in what Sorauf (1957) described as "a process in which interests jockey among themselves to reach the points in governmental decision-making and the influence in the emerging policy."

Conclusion

Policy alternatives chosen on the belief that they will produce some benefit, are often based on invalid or insufficient information. This results in a weak foundation for building a strong program out of the policy. When the foundation fails to hold the structure firmly, we are left feeling cheated. It is up to policy analysts to pave the way for effective policies that alleviate our social problems by advancing knowledge through empirically driven models. Citizens cannot be expected to make demands of their decision-makers wisely if they do not have access to solid information. In other words, they cannot make educated decisions when they are given only half-truths with which to do so. While we know that citizens will choose rationally based on the information that they have available to them, we also know that they will act on information that they believe to be credible and in their best interests (Page and Shapiro, 1992). That information need not be factual or complete to be perceived as valid. All it takes is a key player or players to promote a plausible solution to a problem when the opportunity and timing are right to successfully place an item on the public affairs agenda; when politics, problems, and solutions come together at the right time, legislative action is likely to occur (Kingdon, 1989).

Successful policymaking begins with a clear understanding of the problem that necessitates the policy. Understanding the problems of voting in America is rife with methodological difficulties caused by a variety of phenomena - most notably those that are culturally, ideologically, and paradigmatically based. This chapter identified some of those difficulties that have caused the nature of the problem to remain elusive and argues that much more work is needed before we can claim a complete understanding of the phenomena.

In the next chapter, the particular concerns of the players in the arena within which election reform took place will be discussed. The individual and collective contributions placed into the arena by those attentive to the conditions that made the timing right for a debate on electoral reform are introduced.

Notes

---

[i] Grossman, Harvey. October 26, 2002.. "Punch-card voting system must be retired." Voice of the People Letter, *Chicago Tribune*.

[ii] Caltech/MIT Voting Technology Project. March 2001. Residual Votes Attributable to Technology. Available online at: http://www.hss.caltech.edu/%7Evoting/CalTech_MIT_Report_Version2.pdf, p. 2.

[iii] Brady, Henry E., Justin Buchler, Matt Jarvis and John McNulty. 2001. "Counting all the Votes: The Performance of Voting Technology in the United States." Available online at: www.ucdata.berkeley.edu/new_web/countingallthevotes.pdf, p. 6.

[iv] Figures obtained from the state election authorities in the following states: CA, DE, FL, GA, HI, ID, KS, KY, MO, NV, NY, NC, OK, UT, and WY.

[v] *Bush v. Gore*, 531 U.S. 98 (2000).

[vi] U.S. Commission on Civil Rights, "Voting Rights in Florida 2002: Briefing Summary." Available online at http://www.usccr.gov.

[vii] Institute of Government and Public Affairs. 2002. The Machinery of Democracy: Voting Systems and Ballot Miscounts in Illinois. Available online at: http://www.igpa.uiuc.edu/publications/critIssues/default.htm#democracy.

[viii] Parker, Laura. "Black voters protest over Fla. Election: Some claim they weren't allowed to cast ballots." *Miami Herald*, December 7, 2000, Final Edition: 4A.

[ix] Wilson, Woodrow. 1887. "The Science of Administration." *Political Science Quarterly* 2 (2):197-222.

[x] Taken from the title: Lasswell, Harold Dwight. 1958. *Politics: Who Gets What, When, How.* New York, NY: Meridian Books.

Chapter Three

The Politics of Reform

*"Beyond this circle of seekers after privileges,
individuals and organized minorities…"*
- Walter Lippmann (1889–1974)
U.S. journalist[i]

A Demand For Change

Citizens tend to think of public policy reforms as permanent and total solutions to the problems that we are attempting to solve. The tendency in all of us is to think that once we have designed and implemented the reform measures, we need never worry about the problem again. That is usually not the case, though. Rather, it is limited thinking on our part. The purpose of this book is to clarify the concept of reform, particularly electoral reform, and point out that the American society's working theory of reform is, essentially, flawed. Although we might like to believe that once reform becomes a reality, our problems will disappear, this is no more realistic than to expect that once you clean your home you will never have to clean it again.

Reform measures, no matter how well designed they may be, are constrained by change in terms of both time and circumstance as noted in Chapter 1. In reflecting on the history of electoral reform in the United States, it is apparent that we have reformed many times in years past yet we found ourselves encountering the cry for reform, once again, these many years later at the threshold of the new millennium. Why is it that we never seem to finalize our quest for electoral reform or to create reform policies that can adapt to the changes encountered along the way?

The reason why comprehensive electoral reform eludes us resides in our inherent rational self-interested natures as humans. The demands we make as individuals are rarely ever fully satisfied. Rather, we must continually compromise in order to have any of our demands met in the process of group interaction that characterizes the public affairs arena. This can be clearly demonstrated through analysis of the group process that occurred in recent attempts to prevent another troubled election like that of Election 2000, an election that was, for all intents and purposes, decided by the United States Supreme Court.

The interrelationships and political machinations that are an inherent part of the public policy process resulted in the laying of a foundation for what will, undoubtedly, become another in the series of reforms that have taken place to date in this country with regard to the way in which we choose our elected officials. Those interrelationships and political machinations are innately human activities that occur within the larger context of group dynamics. Societal activities take place within the context of human behaviors. In reading this chapter, it will become clear that complete and total reform is impossible because it requires perfection, something society cannot achieve by virtue of its human components.

Since the game of politics is one played over the division of scarce resources, it produces winners and it produces losers. Ultimately, though, it is rarely a game in which one winner or set of winners takes all. It is a game of negotiation and compromise in which each side must barter and give up something to get something in return. There are winners and losers only by degree in our public affairs system, as was argued in Chapter 1.

This negotiated conflict is the hallmark of the public policy process and the reason why we can never fully achieve reform, if we consider reform to be a change that meets everyone's satisfaction in society. Issues rarely generate policies that are flatly one-sided, ones that reflect only the dominant ideology. Rather, they are like fine works of art that are carved out of the beliefs, demands, and desires of what is often a diverse set of special interests. With multiple participants in the process, the end product is one that is uniquely fashioned.

Three questions must be answered to adequately understand how the Help America Vote Act (HAVA) came to include the particular language that it contains. First, who were the key players who entered the arena of conflict over this set of issues? Second, what were the ideas that each of these actors brought into the arena regarding electoral reform? Finally, what was the set of outcomes that occurred in the form of the HAVA itself? By identifying who made demands, what those demands were, and what the final solution was together both define the process of policy-making and the likelihood that the ultimate policy will be satisfactory to all concerned. In other words, analysis of these three questions not only helps us understand the negotiations and bargaining that brought us to the point we have arrived at, but also helps us to define the future direction the policy will most likely take in its evolutionary cycle. It gives us a sort of predictive power, limited though it may be in the scope of all things, but one that nevertheless gives us a measure of protection against being blindsided by unintended policy consequences. The remainder of this chapter is devoted to answering the first two of those three questions listed above.

Careful inspection of the witnesses and testimony given by them in front of the U.S. House and Senate congressional committees provides a snapshot of some of the key players in the reform game. It is, after all, within the congressional standing committees that the writing of important pieces of legislation takes place (Smith and Deering, 1984). It portrays one historical moment in time, a moment that occurred within the setting of one of the venerable American governmental institutions that house the rules and decision-makers who craft the policies out of the disparate views that come across their radar screens as they search for alternatives to solve societal problems in a manner that will produce the optimal amount of agreement among interests attentive to the issue at hand. In this case, the issue at hand was electoral reform and there were plenty of attentive players.

The amount of media coverage generated by the difficulties of Election 2000 created a substantial amount of interest in electoral reform. A Lexis-Nexis Academic Universe search for newspaper articles was undertaken using the Midwest, Northeast, Southeast, Western, and District of Columbia news sources for the days between November 7, 2000, Election Day, and October 29, 2002, the day the United States Congress passed the HAVA and the same days in years 1998 through 2002. Results of that search, displayed in Table I, indicate that the number of articles pertaining to the two topics of election reform and voting technology (as keywords) dramatically increased from the earlier time frame to that following Election 2000. That increase in newspaper coverage indicates the increase in interest in topics that were of little interest to anyone prior to that point.

The set of circumstances surrounding Election 2000, the media frenzy that surrounded it, and the continuous coverage of topics associated with election reform generated a full set of ideas about how to reform the electoral process. Reform of the electoral system was the topic of conversation across the states from "Joe Sixpack" sitting in his local drinking establishment to CEOs in their boardrooms, all of whom had opinions about how voting would best take place. A recent article that appeared in the *Texas Review of Law and Politics* provides the following list of sixteen concerns that have been identified, at one point or another since Election 2000, regarding changes that should be made to the American electoral process:

- Reform or abolish the Electoral College;
- Establish longer polling place hours;
- Provide better training for polling place workers;
- Create new or better methods of voting, including mail and Internet balloting;
- Establish uniform ballots;
- Ensure more accurate vote-counting mechanisms;

- Revise procedures for conducting recounts, protests, and contests;
- Improve voter education;
- Reform of election day reporting by television;
- Provide for same-day or other novel methods of voter registration;
- Allow weekend or holiday voting;
- Expand the franchise for ex-felons;
- Exact consistent standards for handling situations where voters fail to follow clear instructions;
- Routinely purge voter registration rolls; Provide absentee ballot procedures, including those governing military ballots; and
- Establish measures to eliminate electoral fraud.[ii]

It is important to note that this snapshot does not capture all of the players in the arena. There were key players who were not very visible in the mix of those interested in electoral reform. Those players will be discussed at length later in this chapter. First, though, the chapter engages in a look at the players who came forward to publicly air their concerns.

A Collection Of Perspectives

The list of witnesses who appeared before the two congressional committees convened to debate the merits of the legislation introduced that became the HAVA included a gathering of individuals who were, in one sense, fairly representative of the American citizenry. There were individuals from a variety of walks of life and occupations, with unique perspectives and needs, who came from various socioeconomic backgrounds. On the other hand, that gathering included a combination of public and private special interests that perceived

Table I – Number of Reform/Equipment Newspaper Articles

Topic: Election Reform	Location of News Sources	November 7, 1998 through October 29, 2000	November 7, 2000 and October 29, 2002
	Midwestern	46	314
	Northeastern	59	282
	Southeastern	125	958
	Western	51	298
	District of Columbia	7	167
Topic: Voting Equipment	Location of News Sources	November 7, 1998 through October 29, 2000	November 7, 2000 and October 29, 2002
	Midwestern	7	56
	Northeastern	3	41
	Southeastern	15	220
	Western	14	103
	District of Columbia	2	30

changes in the electoral system as potentially advantageous to them or to society in some manner. They were interests that were already tuned into the process of voting in the U.S. In this sense, this narrowly focused group was not representative of the body of American citizens at all. It was, primarily, the choir that needed no preaching to regarding fixing an ailing system. The only thing the choir members differed on was the way in which to fix that system. As the listing above that appeared in the *Texas Review of Law and Politics* implied, there were quite a few ideas about what the solution was.

So, who were the people and/or groups that came forward and expressed their concerns and preferences of how to fix things? To begin, although partisan differences existed throughout the reform process, there were some genuine, if politically motivated, efforts made to establish the reform process as a bipartisan effort. In the words of Democratic Senator Christopher Dodd (D-CT):

> Recognizing that comprehensive election reform legislation could not be a partisan endeavor, we brought together last fall a bipartisan team of Senators devoted to this issue.[iii]

Efforts made to create a bipartisan effort aimed at election reform were undertaken by The Miller Center of Public Affairs at the University of Virginia. The Miller Center was instrumental in organizing the National Commission on Federal Election Reform, featuring two former American presidents (Jimmy Carter and Gerald R. Ford) among the co-chairs. The Commission was charged with the purpose of investigating allegations of problems in voting across the country and with making recommendations for fixing the ailing system. It published an extensive set of recommendations concerning the election system in a report entitled, "To Assure Pride and Confidence in the Electoral Process."[iv] This report was a primary resource for members of Congress as they debated reform.

In spite of this orchestrated commitment to bipartisanship, remarks made by individual legislators throughout the process, along with amendments introduced, demonstrate clear differences along partisan lines in Congress as to the preferred direction that electoral reform should take. For instance, Democrats favored strong nationalization of the election process while Republicans favored the retention of control over election administration by the individual states.

These differences in preferences with regard to the voting process are consistent with the basic differences in the two parties as they have evolved over the history of the country. Democrats have traditionally favored a strong national governmental presence in the lives of citizens, while Republicans have favored a more limited role for the central government.

A bipartisan effort toward reform meant overriding these differences through a series of trade-offs that each side could live with. This cooperative spirit could contribute significantly toward substantial settlement of controversial issues since the negotiators' settlement expectancies have been demonstrated to be an important component of negotiated outcomes (Neale, 1994.) The move toward a bipartisan effort established the recognition that problem resolution in this case was in the best interests of all decision-makers, regardless of partisan affiliation or personal preference. This is in no way meant to imply that improvement of democracy was driving these preferences. It is quite conceivable that the individual lawmakers, as rational decision-makers, were driven to act toward negotiated settlement in an effort to preserve their political careers. Members of Congress often make decisions that they believe will enhance their chances of re-election (Mayhew, 1974). Actually achieving an enhanced democratic voting process may simply have been a secondary goal in the game of political survival.

Academics were on the list of witnesses who testified on Capitol Hill. Furthermore, they were not unified in their views of what ails the electoral system that produced the problems of Election 2000. In fact, while some researchers point out that there are statistically significant differences in error-propensity across equipment types (Caltech/MIT Project, 2001), one of the congressional witnesses from academia, Larry Sabato of the University of Virginia, urged Congress to proceed cautiously with regard to mandating the replacement of voting equipment and to honor the states' rights to administer their own election systems.[v] This underscores the argument presented in the previous chapter that too little is known about the causes of voting problems to adequately resolve them at this point. As Sabato argued, much more research is necessary to be able to conclusively define the voting problem. So there are two factions or camps within academic circles regarding the nature of election problems: those who wholeheartedly buy into the idea that it is the equipment and those who understand that the complexities of the electoral prospect must be sorted out before an adequate identification of causation can occur. The latter believe we simply do not know enough at this point to make sweeping change a feasible course of action. Yet, the need for empirical analysis of these problems is, generally, not appreciated by society at large as individuals quest to satisfy their unique self-interests. Academics are only one group in an arena of many.

Minority groups were very prominent among the list of witnesses in the congressional committees. Concerned with allegations of the occurrence of discriminatory practices against various minority groups, advocates for election reform from both the public and private sectors appeared as witnesses in an attempt to gain legislative changes that would be favorable to their membership. On the public side, Mary Frances Berry, Chairperson of the United States Commission on Civil Rights, testified before the U.S. Senate Committee on Rules and Administration that a study conducted by the Commission to investigate problems in Florida with Election 2000 that resulted in the ballot recount procedure found that many individuals were turned away from the polls without being able to vote because they had been wrongfully purged from voter registration rolls:

> A combination of restrictive statutory provisions, wide-ranging errors and inadequate and unequal resources in the election process denied countless Floridians the right to vote. The disenfranchisement of Florida's voters fell most harshly on the shoulders of African Americans.[vi]

The U.S. Civil Rights Commission is a public watchdog group, of sorts, in that it is charged with statutory oversight of the Civil Rights Acts. It engages in examination of allegations of abuse of the civil rights laws.

The claims of an unequal protection of voting rights was echoed by other high-powered individuals such as Kweisi Mfume, President of the National Association for the Advancement of Colored People (NAACP), the oldest civil rights organization in the country:

> perhaps millions of voters across the nation were denied their basic right to cast a free vote and to have that vote counted. While the situation in Florida obviously received the most national and media

> attention, and as we just heard from the previous panel that attention was merited, the NAACP believes that Florida is in fact a microcosm of the entire country. Throughout the United States, millions of American citizens were, for one reason or another, not able to cast their vote or have their vote counted.
>
> Furthermore, the NAACP strongly believes that many of the voting irregularities occurred disproportionately in communities of color nationwide, so it was ethnic minority Americans who were, in disparate numbers, excluded from having our voices heard. There was, as best as we have been able to determine, substantial unresolved allegations across the country of massive voter disenfranchisement in African American, Hispanic American, Haitian American and Jewish communities. The election [2000] appeared to have been conducted in such a manner that many of those same communities now believe unequivocally that it was unfair, illegal, immoral and undemocratic.[vii]

Minority groups believed intuitively that there is a fundamental flaw in the structure of the electoral system. The scientific validity of their fears meant little to them. The perception was enough to spur them into action. They were not interested in empirical testing as were the academics. They stood ready to demand assistance in tearing down what they perceived as their barrier to entry into the public affairs arena on an equal footing with others in society. The strategy was to strike while the iron was hot.

Although we tend to treat minority groups as though they are one monolithic force in the public affairs arena, in truth there is a good deal of variety within the ranks of the minority populations of the United States to the point where it has made it difficult for them to build numbers sufficient for gaining a position of power. This can be clearly seen in the struggle by Hispanic-Americans to gain public offices even though they are the fastest growing minority population in the country. Their efforts at gaining a voice in the public affairs arena have been hampered by the fact that although they share a language they are not unified in their politics (De La Garza, Rudolfo O., DiSipio, Garcia, Garcia, and Falcon, 1993).

A variety of minority groups became vocal in their efforts to reform the electoral process in the United State. Hispanic-Americans were among them, but African-Americans and persons with disabilities were, as well, and each of these groups had a distinct and separate list of specific concerns. In some cases, their demands were in sync, as is the case with their apparent shared view of problems with voter registration rolls. In other cases, though, the demands differed. African-Americans and Hispanics were concerned with the disparate placement of what they viewed as problematic voting equipment. This was apparent in the testimony of both Kweisi Mfume of the NAACP and in litigation filed in Federal Court in Illinois in *Black v. McGuffage* in which allegations were made that problematic equipment was disproportionately placed in communities that housed large numbers of African-American and Hispanic voters.[viii] This suit was ultimately settled.

Yet, while placement of voting equipment was shared by both of these groups, Hispanic-Americans were concerned with other difficulties that their members face in trying to vote under the current methods employed. Raul Yzaguirre is the President of the National Council of LaRaza, a private, nonprofit group established in 1968 that represents the rights of Hispanic-Americans. It is the largest constituency-based national Hispanic organization in the United States, with over 270 formal affiliates in 40 states, Puerto Rico, and the District of Columbia. Mr. Yzaguirre, who has led the organization for more than 25 years, pointed out in his testimony before Congress that:

> Spanish-speaking Latino voters received no bilingual assistance at most polling sites. In most precincts the entire election staff spoke only English and count not assist language minority voters. Reports indicate that in some counties, minority voters were asked for photo identification while white voters were not required to show any form of ID. Many polls in disproportionately minority precincts were closed even though voters were still in line; other polls had lines so long that some voters left the polling places without casting their vote.[ix]

Members of these two groups, African-Americans and Hispanic-Americans, while sharing fundamental concerns with the voting system, addressed differing aspects of that system in the demands they placed on the doorstep of Congress. Those concerns were unique to the people who comprised their membership.

Persons with disabilities in the United States are another minority group of sorts. Organizations concerned with advancing the interests and protecting the rights of persons with disabilities also appeared before Congress to present their own set of concerns to decision-makers. While they were concerned with voting equipment and balloting, like their African-American and Hispanic-American counterparts, they were not interested as much in the placement of that equipment as they were in the facility of its usage and issues of privacy for their membership. James C. Dickson, Vice President of the American Association of People With Disabilities, the largest national cross-disability nonprofit organization in the country, testified that persons with disabilities face a wide range of problems with voting and that he, as a blind disabled-American, believed that his vote was not protected on a par with the votes of other citizens. The Americans With Disabilities Act requires that persons with disabilities be allowed to vote with an accommodation such as the services of a sighted reader. In relating his own experiences with the difficulties he has faced in attempting to vote with an accommodation such as this, he stated:

> there is always some level of uncertainty when another person marks your ballot for you. Twice in Massachusetts and once in California, while relying on a poll worker to cast my ballot, the poll worker attempted to change my mind about whom I was voting for. I held firm, but to this day I really do not know if they cast my ballot according to my wishes. Last year's election in Florida caused many Americans to wonder, for the first time, if their vote was tallied for the person they intended to vote for. I, and millions of other American citizens, ask ourselves this question every time we vote. According to a Harris Interactive survey conducted in December 2000, 95% of Americans with disabilities, compared with 86% of the general public, believe that we have a serious problem with how votes are cast and counted.[x]

Another group of organizations, the United Cerebral Palsy Associations, was represented by Mr. Robert R. Williams who appeared before Congress with concerns of accessibility to the polls and bias by poll workers to the table as issues that should be taken into consideration in the crafting of any proposed reform measures. He stressed that decision-makers must take the following into account:

> ...at every election, we hear of at least some people with disabilities either, being turned away from the polls, entirely, or being talked out of voting or registering to vote, for no other reason than they have an obvious disability. In about half the States, people who have had legal guardians appointed for them can not, by law, vote at all. Arid, while on its face, such a prohibition might seem logical and even necessary to protect the integrity of the election process, -the way it is applied is far too broad brush. There are many reasons why a guardian might be appointed for a person with a disability. Many of which have nothing to do with the individual's capacity to comprehend and cast their vote. Yet, in many instances, it is easier for, convicted felons, to have their voting rights restored, than it is for many people with disabilities to legally cast a ballot in some States. I would, therefore, urge this Committee and others in Congress to work with the Administration, State election officials, the disability community and others to closely examine and hopefully develop some reasonable ways of remedying this problem. Our final set of concerns, as I said, is if States and communities are going to receive Federal funding to update and purchase new voting technology, in what ever form that takes, it needs to be accessible.[xi]

These differences of opinion as to what the barrier to entry was constructed of meant a variety of voices and a range of demands coming out of groups commonly grouped together under the monolithic minority label. They underscore the importance of understanding the range of difficulties faced by those who are not included in the mainstream of society. While most of us take the voting process for granted, we tend to overlook the difficulties faced by a number of people in society for whom the act of voting may involve additional burdens. In theory, then, while the vote may be a fundamental participatory vehicle for the majority in the United States, the ability to engage in that form of participatory activity involves varying degrees of difficulty. Certainly, this was something that must be taken into consideration in the design of voting mechanisms.

Concerned with growing public opinion that favored some form of election reform, public officials charged with the administration of elections registered their concerns with what they believed to be some of the potential changes. They appeared before Congress to stress their concerns with feasibility of the various proposed changes. Fixing an ailing system, they believed, could cause difficulties for those charged with implementing the intended changes. Rarely are congressional mandates as easy to put into practice as they would appear to be in the abstract as they are debated in the halls of Congress, as well as in the court of public opinion. Ohio Secretary of State J. Kenneth Blackwell appeared before Congress to urge decision-makers to consider the viewpoints of election administrators before they took action to legally mandate any changes with which they would have to comply. Above all other concerns, Secretary Blackwell pointed out that the states have a difficult time administering elections because the monies for them come out of the "same budgets as money for education, road repairs, mental health services, and welfare, to name a few" of the competing funding needs.[xii] His point that mandates must be accompanied by funding in order for administrators to effectively implement changes is especially important given that downturned budgetary conditions exist across a good number of the states. Without financial assistance from the federal government, election reform would stand little, if any, chance of being implemented successfully. These thoughts were echoed by Doug Lewis, Executive Director of the Election Center, an international association of voter registration and election officials, who pointed out that election administrators and staff work with "almost no resources and almost no understanding by the public of what [they] do".[xiii]

Deborah M. Phillips, Chairman of The Voting Integrity Project, a national non-partisan voter rights organization that studies and documents a wide range of election-related problems, came forward to express her concerns with the failing election system. She stressed that problems with the current voter registration system make maintaining electoral integrity difficult. She also added concerns her organization has with absentee ballots and with the role of election vendors in election integrity and made suggestions that included the following:

> ...centraliz[ing] voter registration list maintenance and to adopt uniform data formats for vital statistics, felony records, tax records, and change of address records...contract with election vendors only after an open, competitive bid process, where vendors are required to meet the same financial and other disclosure standards set for state lottery vendors.[xiv]

As noted earlier in the chapter, not all of the key players in the electoral reform debate were among the most visible of those airing their concerns in the public domain. Interestingly, the group that stood to benefit the most from electoral reform, and one that The Voting Integrity Project was particularly concerned with, was a group that was not very visible in the push for that reform. The equipment manufacturers, the individuals one would expect to see out front given that the production of newer forms of equipment would result in higher profits earned, were remarkably quiet.

Perhaps, the reason for this resides in the focus of all legislative lobbying campaigns that begin with a choice of the type of strategy to employ that will most likely lead to success. As Arnold (1990) demonstrated, groups will adopt either an insider or an outsider approach to legislative lobbying depending, in part, upon the level and type of resources they have at their disposal. Those groups that have the resources necessary to create access to decision-makers often adopt an insider strategy. In these cases, they socialize with those decision-makers and provide any number of resources to them, including campaign contributions.

Although a complete understanding of whether or not this was the case with the equipment manufacturers with regard to election reform is beyond the scope of this work, it seems plausible that with their limited elite membership (the

Federal Election Commission provides a list of only nineteen known vendors of computerized vote tabulation systems, for instance[xv]) and vast economic resources, they could have access to these decision-makers on a regular basis. They would not need to resort to an outsider strategy, the category in which public testimony would fall, to relay their concerns and/or interests to those who could accommodate them. They are regular participants in the public affairs process and might have access by virtue of their continual participation in the arena as insiders to the institutional process.

The extent of insider participation in legislative lobbying efforts is often difficult to track, though. Campaign contributions, for instance, are made indirectly through political action committees and are not necessarily readily discernible without extensive research. For example, the Chief Operating Officer of one of the largest voting equipment manufacturers, Walden O'Dell, of Diebold, Inc., contributed over $5,000 to the Republican National Committee (RNC), according to a report listed on PoliticalMoneyline.Com, an online independent campaign finance tracking organization. The RNC, in turn, contributes to the campaigns of Republican congressional candidates.

Likewise, elections are often rich veins for lawyers to tap into to gain resources. Lawyers make money and reputations off of elections. As pointed out in a *Miami Herald* article shortly after Election 2000, elections can "put big money in the law firm coffers."[xvi] Yet, like the equipment manufacturers, they did not appear as witnesses before the Congressional committees that debated the HAVA. They do, though, contribute heavily to federal candidates for public office. As reported by OpenSecrets.Org, another campaign finance tracking organization, the Association of Trial Lawyers of America contributed $2,813,753 in campaign funds in 2002. Like the equipment manufacturers, lawyers who stand to profit from elections have insider connections that negate the need to consider resorting to outsider tactics designed to garner public support.

The level of influence garnered by that $5,000 made by Mr. O'Dell or by the sums of money given by thousands of private attorneys to the Association of

Trial Lawyers of America Political Action Committee would be impossible to gauge with any accuracy. However, although there is much debate among scholars as to the nature of the influence that campaign contributions can or can't have in the policymaking realm, there appears to be a good deal of support among them for the notion that there is, indeed, influence from contributions (Smith, 1995).[xvii] How far down the chain one must go to determine the point at which the influence begins to shape up at an individual level is open to debate, but one can infer that the connections made between the individuals making those contributions and those to whom the contributions were made will work into a networking scheme that has far-reaching implications for the American public policymaking process.

This lack of visibility on the part of some of the players in the process, certainly, bears greater scrutiny. Identifying the nuances of influence in terms of how they play out does not, however, contribute much to the central argument of this work, namely, that electoral reform is elusive and a myth that public policy is inherently incapable of sustaining for any considerable length of time basis because of temporal and spatial considerations (see Chapter 1). Nonetheless, it is an intriguing question because it underscores the complex nature of the interactions of the various special interests in the arena. Therefore, I leave the task of seeking the causal link between influence election policymaking for the consideration and work of public policy scholars in the future and, indeed, encourage this line of inquiry.

So far, we have looked at a variety of actors in the process, all of whom had some proposed solution to fixing the problem of voting in the United States that they brought with them into the decision-making arena. There were, though, individuals who were clearly against many of the proposed changes and appeared before Congress to signal the danger in moving too quickly to implement legislation that is based on knowledge gleaned from agreement rather than that which is scientifically validated.

Although the U.S. Commission on Civil Rights was represented by Mary Frances Berry, Chairman of the Commission, another Commission member also appeared before Congress. This member dissented from the majority opinion of the Commission regarding conclusions it had arrived at following Election 2000 and the status of equal protection of the vote for many members of minority populations. She appeared to actively lobby against some of the proposed changes. Abigail Thernstrom is a Commission member who is a political scientist by training and a senior fellow at the Manhattan Institute in New York. She is also a highly regarded member of the Massachusetts state board of education. Dr. Thernstrom appeared before Congress and testified that her experience as a member of the Commission led her to believe the Commission has hindered progress on the road to racial equality in the United States more than it has helped. She argued that information provided by the Commission's Chairman, Mary Frances Berry, was not garnered in a fair and impartial manner and that the Commission was, in her opinion, a "national embarrassment" by virtue of a number of practices which she outlined in her testimony. Chairman Berry stated the following in her testimony regarding the practices of its hearings and briefings into the events in the State of Florida following Election 2000 made:

> a mockery of intellectual inquiry... and, as a consequence, the work is shoddy and ideologically-driven. Preliminary findings are issued without following basic scholarly or collegial process. Reports are leaked to the press before being give to Commissioners...Fear of input from affected parties in Florida, from scholars outside the Commission, and from Commissioners themselves drove a process that lacked even bare-bones integrity. And a corrupt process insured a worthless result.[xviii]

In another appearance before Congress in hearings held regarding election reform, Dr. Thernstrom reiterated her objections to the majority report issued by the U.S. Commission on Civil Rights, but taking things a bit further by introducing the idea that partisan politics was driving the allegations made in that report:

> Nothing is more fundamental to American democracy than the right to vote and to have that vote properly counted. Allegations of

disfranchisement are the fertile ground in which a dangerous distrust of American political institutions thrives. When those allegations are driven by partisan interests and have no basis in fact, distrust, alienation and cynicism have been needlessly and irresponsibly fostered. Democracies are always fragile. Today, the Commission eagerly labels as illegitimate the results of the 2000 election; tomorrow, true democrats, across party lines, will rue the day it did so.[xix]

Dr. Thernstrom's appearance before Congress followed an appearance by Dr. John Lott, resident scholar of the American Enterprise Institute, a large well-respected think tank located in Washington, DC, who appeared before Congress several months earlier and presented results of his research into the events of Florida in Election 2000. Dr. Lott stressed that the issues of discrimination raised by a variety of groups were unfounded based on his own careful statistical analysis of the electoral data in that:

Disturbing claims of discrimination have also been raised after the 2000 Presidential Election. African-American ballots were said to be spoiled at higher rates than the ballots of other groups. [While] Representative Conyers' bill notes that there is overwhelming evidence that disparate procedures and antiquated machinery have a disproportionate racial impact...it is difficult to accept the commission's conclusion that discrimination was unintentional and surely not intentional, unless one believes that black democratic county election supervisors were responsible for higher non-voted ballot rates by African-American voters.[xx]

Chapter 2 engaged in a discussion of the difficulties involved in researching electoral matters in a scientific manner. This is a crucial point when weighing the concerns expressed by a variety of entities, particularly when there is disagreement as to the validity of those concerns. It is clear from the two opposing sets of testimony that ideology played an important role in and among the views of these various groups of actors and is not simply a methodological difficulty that researchers face that interfered with their ability to accurately assess the set of conditions comprising the electoral reform phenomena. Obviously, there were conflicting opinions as to what constituted the reality of events surrounding Election 2000, which translated into a varied set of proposed changes to the voting process in the United States. Arriving at a measure aimed at reforming the process would not be an easy task given these differences in perspectives.

Where was the general public throughout this process? Apparently University of Chicago law professor Richard Epstein (2001) was right in his intuitive belief that interest in voting problems ceased when the Supreme Court made its ruling in *Bush v. Gore*. Although everyone had an opinion in the days and months following Election 2000, interest in the voting process did appear to wane among the citizenry. Table II shows answers to the questions posed to a nationwide sampling of adults at two points in time, December 2000 and November 2001, in a *USA TODAY*/CNN/Gallup poll that reveal a change in public opinion over time with regard to the problems associated with voting in the United States. While only 15.0% of those polled had a great deal of confidence in the voting system in December of 2000, that figure climbed to 21% by November of 2001. Conversely, while 35.0% indicated very little confidence in the system in 2000, the figure had dropped to 25.0% not quite a year later.

A most striking difference in opinion is reflected in the responses to the question specifically regarding election reform. While a total of 67.0% of those polled favored either a complete overhaul (39.0%) or a major reform (28.0%) of the voting system in 2000, that figure dropped substantially to a total of only 35.0% the next year. Time forces a reconsideration of the concerns that we hold. Voting was a major concern for a short duration of time after Election 2000 but was replaced by more recent events. Empirical evidence, therefore, suggests that while citizens did not forget their concerns about voting problems, they no longer saw them as pressing.

This decline in interest among the general public was an important component of the reform effort, albeit, an indirect one. An inattentive audience does not seek representation in the legislative process (Arnold, 1990). In the absence of effort to push the preferences of the majority agenda, an attentive minority will be able to successfully push its own agenda.

In this chapter, the electoral reform concerns of a variety of special interests have been examined. Evidence of the specific nature of those concerns as a varied set of focal points was presented that highlighted the fact that the influence that each group has both separately and in tandem with the others is quite a complex matter. While all groups exhibited a unified concern for the democratic ideal of equality, rational self-interest dictates the specific demands made to decision-makers that made crafting the actual public policy reform measure a difficult undertaking. The next chapter engages in a discussion of the outcomes of the interactions of those groups in the public policymaking process that became the HAVA. As will become clear, while portions of the concerns of each group were accommodated, none of the groups came away completely satisfied with the election reform measure passed by Congress. The citizen groups did not prevail over business, completely, but neither did business walk away without concessions.[xxi]

Conclusion

This chapter provided an overview of the concerns and activities undertaken by a variety of players in the public process in their attempt to clearly define the problem as they worked toward arriving at voting reform. Players in the reform arena such as academics, politicians and political parties, lawyers, minority groups, administrators, and the citizenry at large were, and continue to be, at odds in the struggle to identify both the complexities of the problem and an adequate solution to it as they struggle for positioning in their battle to implement equal protection in voting. While a reform measure was crafted and is currently in the process of being implemented, the contribution of this measure in enhancing a fundamental process of participatory democracy is far from certain. This concept will be explored in the next chapter in more depth.

Table II – Public Opinion on Electoral Reform

	2001	2000
How much confidence do you have in the system in which votes are cast and counted in this country?		
A great deal	21	15
Quite a lot	20	15
Some	32	32
Very little	25	35
None	1	2
No opinion	1	1
Do you think the system in which votes are cast and counted in this country is in need of [a complete overhaul, major reforms, minor reforms, no reforms]?		
Complete overhaul	19	28
Major reforms	24	39
Minor reforms	45	27
No reforms	9	4
No opinion	3	2
Which of these statements do you think best describes the situation that occurred as a result of the 2000 presidential election last year – [it was a constitutional crisis, it was a major problem for the country but was not a crisis, it was a minor problem for the country, it was not a problem for the country at all]?		
Constitutional crisis	7	17
Major problem	35	46
Minor problem	42	25
Not a problem	13	9
No opinion	3	3

©2000, 2001 The Gallup Organization. All rights reserved. Reprinted with permission.

Notes

[i] The Essential Lippmann, pt. 3, sct. 6 (1982). "The New Congress," *New York Herald Tribune* (December 8, 1931).

[ii] Uhlmann, Michael M. 2001. "Federalism and Election Reform." *Texas Review of Law and Politics* V6:497-498.

[iii] Remarks by Senator Christopher Dodd (D-CT) on the Congressional Record, February 13, 2002.

[iv] National Commission on Federal Election Reform. 2002. *To Assure Pride and Confidence in the Electoral Process.* Washington, DC: Brookings Institute.

[v] Testimony by Larry J. Sabato, Director of the University of Virginia Center for Governmental Studies, before the U.S. Senate Committee on Rules and Administration, June 27, 2001.

[vi] Testimony before the U.S. Senate Committee on Rules and Administration of Mary Frances Berry, Chairperson, U.S. Commission on Civil Rights on Wednesday, June 27, 2001.

[vii] Testimony before the U.S. Senate Committee on Rules and Administration of Kweisi Mfume, President, The National Association for the Advancement of Colored People, on Wednesday, June 27, 2001.

[viii] *Black v. McGuffage*, No. 01-01C208 No. 01 C796, 209 F. Supp 2d 889 (March 29, 2002).

[ix] Testimony before the U.S. Senate Committee on Rules and Administration of Raul Yzaguirre, President, National Council of LaRaza, on Wednesday, June 27, 2001.

[x] Testimony before the U.S. House of Representatives Judiciary Committee of James C. Dickson, Vice President, American Association of People With Disabilities, on Wednesday, December 5, 2001.

[xi] Testimony before the U.S. Senate Committee on Rules and Administration of Robert R. Williams of the United Cerebral Palsy Associations, on March 14, 2001.

[xii] Testimony before the U.S. Senate Committee on Rules and Administration of Ohio Secretary of State J. Kenneth Blackwell, on Wednesday, June 27, 2001.

[xiii] Testimony before the U.S. Senate Committee on Rules and Administration of Doug Lewis, Executive Director, The Election Center, March 14, 2001.

[xiv] Testimony before the U.S. Senate Committee on Rules and Administration of Deborah M. Phillips, Chairman of The Voting Integrity Project, March 14, 2001.

[xv] That figure is available online from the Federal Election Commission. 2002b. Known Vendors of Computerized Vote Tabulation Systems. Available online at: www.fec.gov/elections.html.

[xvi] Kirscher-Goodman, Cindy. "Lawyers Felt the pull of Politics & Business." *Miami Herald*. December 4, 2000, 2B.

[xvii] See Smith, Richard A. 1995. "Interest Group Influence in the U.S. Congress." *Legislative Studies Quarterly*. XX:1:89-139 for a review of the conflict among scholars over the causal chain of interest group influence in Congress.

[xviii] Testimony before the U.S. House of Representatives Judiciary Committee of Abigail Thernstrom, Commissioner, U.S. Commission on Civil Rights, April 11, 2002.

[xix] Testimony before the U.S. Senate Committee on Rules and Administration of Abigail Thernstrom, on Wednesday, June 27, 2001.

[xx] Testimony before the U.S. House of Representatives Judiciary Committee of John Lott, Resident Scholar, American Enterprise Institute, December 5, 2001.

[xxi] This supports the earlier work of Jeffrey M. Berry (2002) who argued that citizen and business groups have become much more competitive in recent years and that even though citizen groups have made great strides in accomplishing their legislative goals, business groups are still a viable force in the political arena.

Chapter Four
Road To Reform

"Every reform, however necessary, will by weak minds be carried to an excess, which will itself need reforming."
- Samuel Taylor Coleridge

Crafting A Compromise

> The modernization of [the voting] system will help ensure that each voter who wants to vote is given that opportunity while ensuring that each vote is counted only once. This bill will restore confidence and renew the trust of the American people in the election process.[i]

These were the words of U.S. House of Representatives Speaker Dennis Hastert in his announcement of the passage of the Help America Vote Act (HAVA). This legislation was an attempt to satisfy the concerns of both individuals and special interest groups in response to the problems with elections in the United States brought to light in the aftermath of Election 2000. The measure was billed to be one of sweeping change to the electoral process. What constitutes sweeping change, though, and why would members of the U.S. Congress want citizens to believe they had crafted legislation that had created sweeping change?

Political scientists have long known that some public policy proposals are so compelling that legislators feel they must take decisive action. Yet, in situations where the problem involved is complex, citizens may not be capable of discerning what the best course of action may be to produce the outcomes that they desire (Arnold, 1990). The HAVA is one more example, albeit a very prominent and expensive one, of a policy measure that superficially appears to have what it takes to resolve a societal problem, but which upon closer inspection fails to live up to its billing. Of the sixteen proposed suggestions for change in the voting process listed in Chapter 3, only a portion were actually tangibly addressed by the HAVA. Furthermore, while the majority of that group of measures included in the HAVA were mandated upon the states, several key provisions were left up to the discretion of the individual states whether to implement them or not.

In quite a significant way, the HAVA, while satisfying various special interests, was a ceremonious way for the members of Congress to pass the responsibility for decision-making on some of the more controversial changes onto the individual states. It was a masterfully crafted piece that served two purposes, therefore. It superficially satisfied many of the interested parties involved in the conflict over what appropriately constituted a reformed electoral system and, at the same time, it shifted the burden of final decision-making regarding the scope and direction of reform to each individual state.

Debating the overhaul of existing voting laws has kept state legislators busy since Election 2000. As shown in Table III, there have been a total of 5,295 pieces of election reform legislation introduced in state legislatures throughout the country since Election 2000 occurred. Of that total number of proposals, 688 have been signed into law and, as of this writing, there are over 200 pieces of existing legislation still pending (National Conference of State Legislatures - http://www.ncsl.org/programs/legman/elect/taskfc/03billsum.htm).

The move to change the arena of conflict and shift the responsibility for electoral reform is not an altogether unexpected one. We know that legislators make attempts to anticipate how their actions might be used against them and often adjust their voting in an effort to forestall any future electoral problems (Kingdon, 1989).

One interesting note, here, is that the figures available for 2001 and 2002 indicate legislative measures taken prior to the passage of the HAVA. Obviously,

Table III – State Legislative Reform Measures Introduced

	2001	2002	2003	Total
Number of Bills Introduced	2,088	1,555	1,652	5,295
Number of Bills Signed into Law	321	171	196	688
Number of Bills Still Pending	-	-	271	271

Source: National Conference of State Legislatures

the states initiated actions on their own to try to resolve the problems brought to light by Election 2000. They did not need to be prompted by the federal government to actively engage this issue. While it is unlikely that those problems would have been resolved in each of the states without intervention by the federal government, one thing is clear. The states were already actively engaged in attempting to alleviate the problems with voting prior to any mandated activity by the federal government.

Legislation introduced in the states varied according to the uniquely perceived needs of each state. This is apparent in the overview of the state election reforms enacted in 2001 and 2002 listed in Table IV compiled by the National Conference of State Legislators.[ii] The reform measures vary widely and result in a patchwork of uniquely tailored voting procedures in the individual states, a composite which many proponents of federal election reform measures hoped would be replaced by greater uniformity across the country as a whole.

According to the enabling clause of the HAVA, this Act, passed as a bipartisan measure in House Resolution 3295, is a measure designed to:

> establish a program to provide funds to States to replace punch card voting systems, to establish the Election Assistance Commission to assist in the administration of Federal elections and to otherwise provide assistance with the administration of certain Federal election laws and programs, to establish minimum election administration standards for States and units of local government with responsibility for the administration of Federal elections, and for other purposes.[iii]

The broad wording of this HAVA enabling clause belies the complex nature of the details contained in the text of the Act itself. As with a good many public acts, the legalese that the HAVA is written in makes analysis a difficult task. A careful review of this Act discloses a package whose contents are the result of an orchestrated game of negotiation and compromise among interested parties. The HAVA was carefully worded to strategically maneuver the outcome to eliminate the potential for further conflict in a specific arena, at least in the short term.

The following pages provide an account of some of the important pieces of information fed into the political environment by the various actors concerned with this matter. Again, they portray a process in which there were winners, as well as losers, but only by degrees. No single group, individual, or entity came away from this process a total victor and, therein, rests the foundation that future reform will be built upon at some point down the road. As noted in the first chapter, as long as there are those who feel they have received less than what they desire out of the pot of scarce resources in the public policy process, there exists the potential for future conflict as individuals and groups attempt to equalize the resource levels in those specific policies.

The recent attempt to reform electoral policy in the United States is no exception to the rule. It is clear that there is a reasonable degree of potential for conflict with regard to the future status of the electoral reform policy measures recently instituted. Reform breeds its own future reform by its very nature. The HAVA will not be an exception to that rule.

In the previous chapter, two of the three questions posed as important to an in-depth understanding of the reform policy process and the likelihood that the reform measure adopted will be successful were examined. Those questions were, who were the key actors and what were the ideas that each of them brought into the arena regarding electoral reform? This chapter addresses the third question posed, namely, what was the set of outcomes that occurred? The specific measures included in the HAVA, examined against the set of key ideas and demands placed on decision-makers regarding changes to the electoral process in the United States, helps us to understand the negotiations and bargaining that brought us to the point we have arrived at. More importantly, though, it helps us to define the future direction that the policy will most likely take in its evolutionary cycle. It gives us a sort of predictive power, limited though it may be in the scope of all things, but one that nevertheless gives us a measure of protection against being blindsided by unintended policy consequences.

Voting equipment was a major focus of a number of the special interest players in the reform game. Members of the academic community, for instance, came forward with the results of their studies on a variety of topics associated with the problems of Election 2000. I noted in the previous chapter that one set of researchers indicated they had evidence to suggest that the voting equipment played a major role in contributing to those problems. Based on their research findings, they issued a plea to decision-makers to replace discard punch card voting equipment across the country with newer forms of equipment. This information was disseminated into the information environment through websites on the Internet and through press releases distributed by Caltech and MIT Universities. Stephen Ansolabehere, a member of that research team, also brought those findings to the House Senate Committee of Congress.[iv]

Other researchers, though, attempted to dispel allegations brought forth by some groups after Election 2000 that punch card systems were to be found in disproportionate numbers among precincts in which there were predominantly nonwhite voters. They claimed to have evidence indicating that, in fact, while punch card systems were the norm in Hispanic-American populated precincts, direct record electronic systems and lever machines were more the norm in both African-American and white precincts.[v] In reality, although these two issues, the reliability of punch card systems and the placement of those systems, are separate issues, they fused together at some point where it became impossible to separate

Table IV – Electoral Reform Across the States

Issue	States that enacted new laws in 2001 and 2002
New Voting Equipment	Arizona, California, Florida, Georgia, Idaho, Indiana, Kentucky, Maryland, Michigan, Minnesota, Missouri, Rhode Island, South Dakota, Utah, West Virginia
Voting Equipment Standards & Procedures	Georgia, Idaho, New Mexico, Pennsylvania, Texas, Utah, Vermont
Ban on Punch Cards	Florida, Indiana, Iowa, North Carolina, Texas, Wisconsin
Registration – New or improved centralized voter database	Colorado, Florida, Indiana, Kansas, Mississippi, Oregon, Pennsylvania, Rhode Island, South Dakota, Washington
Registration – Improved list maintenance and purging procedures	Georgia, Indiana, Kansas, Kentucky, Louisiana, Maine, Maryland, Mississippi, Missouri, Montana, Oklahoma, Pennsylvania, Rhode Island, South Dakota, Texas, Virginia, Washington
Voter Intent	Arkansas, California, Florida, Mississippi, Missouri*, Nevada, North Carolina, Ohio, Pennsylvania, South Dakota, Tennessee, Virginia, Washington, Wyoming
Recount Procedures	Arkansas, California, Colorado, Florida, Iowa, Kansas, Nevada, North Carolina, Oklahoma, South Dakota, Tennessee, Texas, Utah, Virginia, Washington, Wyoming
Absentee Voting Procedures	Alaska, Arkansas, California, Colorado, Florida, Georgia, Idaho, Indiana, Iowa, Kentucky, Louisiana, Maine, Maryland, Minnesota, Missouri, Nebraska, Nevada, New Jersey, New Mexico, New York, North Carolina, North Dakota, Ohio, Oklahoma, Pennsylvania, Rhode Island, South Carolina, Tennessee, Utah, Vermont, Virginia, Washington, West Virginia
Provisional Ballots	Colorado, Florida, Indiana, Maryland,

	Missouri, Nebraska, Utah, Vermont, Virginia, Wyoming
Poll Workers – Increased pay, training, and/or recruitment	Alabama, Arkansas, Colorado, Florida, Georgia, Indiana, Iowa, Kentucky, Louisiana, Maryland, Michigan, Mississippi, Missouri, Montana, Nebraska, New Jersey, New Mexico, North Carolina, Pennsylvania, Rhode Island, South Carolina, Texas, Virginia, West Virginia, Wisconsin
Polling Place and Voting Machine Accessibility for Elderly/Disabled Voters	Alaska, Arizona, California, Georgia, Indiana, Kentucky, Missouri, Nevada, New Jersey, New Mexico, North Carolina, Ohio, Pennsylvania, Utah, Virginia, West Virginia
Improved Voter Education	Arizona, Arkansas, California, Florida, Georgia, Indiana, Iowa, Kansas, Kentucky, Maine, Minnesota, Missouri, Montana, Nevada, New Jersey, North Carolina, North Dakota, Oregon, South Dakota, Texas
Legislative Task Forces/Study Commissions/Interim Committees on Election Reform	Arkansas, Florida, Georgia, Hawaii, Kentucky, Maryland, Montana, Nebraska, New Hampshire, North Dakota, Ohio, Oregon, Pennsylvania, Texas, Virginia

Source: National Conference of State Legislatures[vi]

one from the other. Punch card systems became a symbol of racial and ethnic discrimination in the voting process. Once this occurred, nothing short of punch card demise would satisfy certain special interest groups, particularly those whose membership included African-Americans and Hispanics.

Interestingly, the U.S. House Judiciary Congressional Committee report on voting irregularity in Election 2000 was vague with regard to evidencing the problems of voting equipment. Although there are numerous mentions of voting equipment in the report, it states that:

> While statisticians have estimated that as many as 2% of all ballots cast for the office of President nationwide were discarded because of machine errors and voter errors, this report attempts to catalogue from states in which the data is available the actual number of

discarded or unrecorded ballots. The numbers are staggering. At least 1,276,916 voters in 31 states and the District of Columbia had their votes discarded with no vote for President, greater than the difference in the popular vote between Al Gore and George W. Bush. In fact, in at least four states, the number of unrecorded ballots was greater than the margin of victory of the prevailing candidate in that state and could have resulted in a switch in electoral votes between candidates...It appears that the problems with machines and voter error may have been exacerbated by untrained and underpaid poll workers (House Judiciary Report - http://election2000.stanford.edu/electionreporthouse.pdf, pp. 14-15).

The only finding in the report that pertains to voting equipment is, therefore, linked directly to human error. The report specifically indicates that training levels and other individual demographic forces account for voting error. One of the primary documents available to individual Judiciary Committee members, the report prepared by their own staff, and used to weigh the evidence on voting irregularities and concerns in the testimony of the various witnesses who appeared before them failed to provide hard-hitting details of the problem of voting equipment, specifically punch cards. This may account for the fact that the provisions with regard to voting equipment contained in the HAVA, itself, were not mandatory. Mandates only applied to states when they accepted funding, as well.

The issue of potential vote fraud was also something that academics were concerned about. The potential for this occurrence was linked to faulty voter registration systems. Arguing that faulty registration systems can be found in "any region of the country," Larry Sabato from the University of Virginia pointed out that accomplishing reform meant resolving a very complex set of problems rather than a simple one that could be alleviated with a simple fix.[vii] He urged Congress in his testimony not to place nationwide mandates on voting systems because each state is different and has its own set of unique needs that would be difficult to accommodate within a federal policy. He pressed, instead, for a concentration on educating the public toward enhanced participation beginning with funding programs such as the University of Virginia's Youth Leadership Initiative that strives to improve on civic education by working with middle and high school students. Of course, at the same time this would benefit society, it would also benefit the University of Virginia.

Overall, academics were concerned, essentially, with three of the sixteen problems identified on the list that appeared in the *Texas Law Review* article noted above: improving voting equipment, enhancing voter registration systems to cut down on voter fraud, and working to educate the youth of America toward increasing their participation in the electoral arena. Other special interest groups supported the lobbying efforts of academics, at various points in the reform process that helped them realize, at least, a portion of success with achieving the reforms they sought and, in fact, to go beyond their concerns at times, as will become clear below.

Title I of the HAVA pertains to voting equipment and, therefore, to one of the demands made by several groups. Specifically, the HAVA identifies the punch card voting technology as the particular type of equipment eligible for replacement reimbursement under the Act, but it does not mandate that states actually replace the equipment. It allows the states some latitude in their choice of voting equipment by providing three options open to them regarding punch card equipment.

First, the language of the HAVA allows states a series of choices. They may opt to replace punch card equipment with a non-punch card type of system. Those states choosing this option will be required to provide assurances that the equipment being replaced is from jurisdictions that used punch card equipment in Election 2000 in order to be eligible to receive a one-time lump-sum payment of matching funds for replacement of the equipment. Those matching funds are limited to $6,000 per precinct employing the equipment. There are also deadlines that must be met for eligibility purposes.

The second option available through the HAVA to the states with respect to voting equipment is that they may opt to make adjustments to their existing punch card equipment to enhance the performance of that equipment. If they choose this option, they are eligible for a one-time payment of matching funds for replacement of the equipment totaling $2,000 per precinct employing the equipment. Again, there are deadlines associated with eligibility for this option. Additionally, the value of making adjustments to existing equipment by installing error detection capability to the equipment has not been tested enough to fully understand whether this, in fact, alleviates the equal protection problem that many groups claim. Much further testing is needed to establish the success rate in reducing the residual voting error achieved by this type of technology (Kropf, 2003).

Finally, the states may choose to do nothing about their equipment. This may, ultimately, be the most problematic option for the states since they potentially become the target of lawsuits by groups that feel their members have been unfairly discriminated against by election authorities in those states on the basis that they failed to protect all of the votes equally. This has been the basis for the suits that have already been filed in several states. As a matter of fact, various legal groups have come forth and vowed to defend the voting rights of all citizens. Members of the legal community also, then, play a continuing key role in the reform process.

The Lawyers' Committee for Civil Rights Under Law, a private, nonprofit and nonpartisan legal organization, has vowed to "consider all available and appropriate legal remedies under state and federal law" in its pledge to protect those rights.[viii] Ultimately, this could prove to be even more costly to the states if they choose not to replace or adjust their equipment. Most state election boards are composed of equal numbers of partisans who could, conceivably, be divided in their support for defending suits of this nature. Even if they elect to settle the suits and arrive at a compromise measure, settlements involve costs as well, ones that can often be greater than would have been the case if the suit had played out at litigation. This would be the case, for instance, if lawyers for the states fail to adequately assess the probability of winning the suit or if the states that are facing budgetary crises, as so many are in today's economic climate, do not have sufficient funds to sustain a lengthy legal battle. Perhaps this was one of the considerations by the members of the Illinois Board of Elections in entering into a settlement agreement in the lawsuit filed against it in regard to its authorization of the placement of certain voting equipment (*Black v. McGuffage*). Although it now appears that the equipment will be replaced because of the suit filed by the American Civil Liberties Union, given that technological change has been a major part of the voting process in America, chances are that the equipment would have been replaced eventually even without the suit having been filed. As it is, the older equipment will still be in place during the 2004 presidential election. The settlement did not change that.

Another dilemma the states face in attempting to live up to the requirements of the HAVA with regard to the replacement or adjustment of equipment has to do with costs, as well. If a state chooses either of the first two options, replacing or adjusting equipment, it is eligible for matching funds only. That means that the state must come up with the funds necessary for replacing or adjusting the existing equipment. In a downturned economic climate, some states could face a real hardship if they choose to replace the equipment. When dollars and jobs are scarce, voting equipment may not be a top priority to the average person who may be more concerned about surviving the economic hard times than with voting systems and elections. In making a costly decision, lawmakers could potentially be forced into a posture that they will have to justify to taxpayers who will be voting on that new equipment and could, conceivably, punish those decision-makers by voting them out of their positions.

A recent report of a survey commissioned by the Pew Charitable Trust of state lawmakers from across the country indicated that 65% of them felt their states had lost ground over the past couple of years, particularly with regard to lost jobs and the economy, in general (Princeton Survey Review Associates, Inc. - http://www.stateline.org/specialreport/Pew%20State%20Legislators%20%238288 .pdf). The incidence of this sentiment by legislators is even stronger in large states, those with populations in excess of six million, where 75.0% of the legislators surveyed indicated they felt their states had suffered economically and anticipated that conditions would continue to deteriorate in the foreseeable future.

Given this evidence of the pressure created by a set of constrained economic conditions in which state legislators will be forced to make policy decisions, opting between the trustee role and the politico one, in Davidson's (1969) terms, when making those decisions, it is a distinct possibility that costs born by the taxpayers will be a consideration worth deliberating over that may, ultimately, lead them into a delegate role voting in accord with their perception of voters' preference. On the other hand, though, the hype over what has successfully been presented as problematic and malfunctioning equipment to the general public, along with pressure by equipment manufacturers, may be enough to tip the scales in favor of replacing equipment in many of the affected states.

So, although decision-makers in these states must labor over whether to replace equipment, adjust existing equipment, or open their states up to possible legal action if they choose to do nothing, there is no easy choice to be made. No matter which option they choose, there are potential consequences. Although the replacement of voting equipment is not a mandate of the HAVA, in a practical sense, it may as well have been. The equipment manufacturers have already gained a great deal from the states that rushed to appease what they perceived as a demand by the citizenry for equipment change and the manufacturers may continue to profit, since replacing equipment may be the least costly measure to the majority of the states making that decision.

Interestingly, the HAVA may force states into making creative institutional changes in order to comply with the HAVA. In Coles County, Illinois, a county that relies on punch cards, the County Board Offices and Rules Committee took steps to reduce the number of its polling places in order to cut down on the number of machines that will be necessary to replace the punch card systems (Fopay, 2003). While this may cut down on the amount of money needed to comply with the provisions of the HAVA related to replacement/adjustment of voting equipment, it may violate another provision of the HAVA, namely, that which seeks to ensure that voters with disabilities not face additional hardships in attempting to vote. If there are fewer polling places, it is conceivable that it is more difficult for persons with disabilities to get to their polling places.

In addition to the above set of conditions regarding voting equipment, all equipment must be compliant with existing laws protecting the rights of the elderly and disabled. Essentially, the wording pertaining to the rights of the elderly and the disabled, as well as the wording that stresses the importance of accommodating citizens with limited English proficiency in the HAVA is designed to ensure that persons who fall into one of these three groups would be able to vote regardless of their unique status as citizens. The emphasis on these particular sections in the HAVA was an attempt to satisfy the special interest groups that represented the elderly, the disabled, and the immigrant population for whom English is a second language and who face difficulties in attempting to vote using a ballot that includes instructions written in English only. Groups concerned with the rights of the disabled and/or language-hampered such as the United Cerebral Palsy Associations and the Puerto Rican Legal Defense and Education Fund, Inc., lobbied Congress hard, including preparing oral and written testimony, for the changes that they, ultimately, succeeded in obtaining. In the case of language requirements, the HAVA requires that assistance be provided to enable those with limited proficiency in the English language to be able to vote adequately and have that vote counted.

Although the HAVA includes these provisions that appear to benefit persons with disabilities and/or English language deficiencies, in reality it does little more than emphasize the importance of enforcing existing laws that prohibit discriminatory practices against voters who, due to physical, mental, or cultural limitations, are not able to exercise their right to equal access in voting. The Americans With Disabilities Act, the Voting Accessibility for the Elderly and Handicapped Act, and the Voting Rights Language Assistance Act of 1992, all represent legislation that was passed to clarify and/or extend the Voting Rights

Act of 1965. With regard to the issues confronting persons with disabilities and their ability to exercise their right to vote, the HAVA is largely symbolic.

An apparently troubled voter registration system across the country also took center stage in the reform process. Journalists, during the weeks that followed the coverage of the recount process in Florida after Election 2000, raised concerns with the lack of a clear set of uniform standards regarding the decision of what constitutes a spoiled ballot, and the question of when a person is entitled to demand the right to vote in the event of uncertainty over proper voting registration prompted Congress to include the specific language contained in Title V of the HAVA. This section sets the minimum standards that mandate the establishment of a statewide voter registration system on each state and charges states that receive funding under the HAVA with establishing a benchmark for voting system performance across its local jurisdictions. It does not, however, require that states designate specific criteria for determining spoiled ballots. That is left largely up to the individual states to define.

The voter registration changes mandated by the HAVA were the result, primarily, of the combined pressure stemming from journalists and academics. These changes will mean that state voter registration systems must be maintained and updated on a regular basis to ensure that the records it contains are as accurate as possible. In essence, states are required to meet basic compliance with the National Voter Registration Act of 1993 which limits registrants from being purged from each state's system to those who have not voted in two or more consecutive general elections for federal office and who have failed to respond to official notice of removal (Pub. L. 107-252). As such, there will always be a time lag that causes distortion in the number of registered voters across the state. Numbers of registered voters maintained by the states will never be completely accurate, HAVA or not. Furthermore, since the mandate for statewide registration of voters does not include linkage between and among the fifty states, there is no way to track interstate changes. Since people routinely move from state-to-state, especially in a time when corporate transfers are commonplace, this could be a potentially troubling gap in the ability to track voters in this country. At the very least, there is no way to adequately assess the changes in voting patterns that may result from the migratory habits of U.S. citizens in this new millennium.

As Deborah M. Phillips of The Voting Integrity Project noted, finding some way of cross-checking voter registrations between states may be the "next logical step," implying that future legislation to fine-tune the reform will be necessary.[ix] Practitioners in the public affairs arena, then, are aware on some level that reform is ephemeral even before the measures that bring about that reform become a reality.

Advancement toward adequate educational efforts that could benefit U.S. voters was written into the HAVA. Academics and administrators charged with oversight of the electoral process who wanted to see improvement of that process take place were rewarded by the inclusion of language making funding for education of voters and election staff a reality.

Concerns about absentee ballots, particularly for military and other citizens stationed overseas, were raised in testimony before the congressional committees. The HAVA establishes guidelines that must be adhered to regarding the ability of persons who are overseas at the time of the election to vote and have their vote counted. Since this was a thorny part of the conflict in Election 2000, careful consideration was given to protecting the votes of military personnel serving their country. As a result, there will now be mandates for voting assistance to military personnel that include such things as voting assistance officers to be assigned by the Department of Defense and made available to members of the armed services to answer questions, register to vote, provide information, and so on during a reasonable period of time prior to general elections when those voters may be preparing absentee ballots. The Inspector General of the Department of Defense will also be required to furnish yearly evaluative progress reports on the voting assistance process to Congress for their oversight. Military personnel, post-Election 2000, post-911 disaster, in a year that witnessed rapid advancement toward military action in the Middle East, were included as a significant portion of the HAVA. Failure to take them into account within the confines of the particular set of events in America would have potentially generated much controversy in the arena of public opinion.

In this sense, passage of the HAVA effectively served to diffuse a societal ticking bomb. It changed the arena of conflict, moving it out of the hands of Congress, and placing it squarely on the shoulders of the individual states. In light of the U.S. Supreme Court's majority opinion in *Bush v. Gore*, it did so appropriately since the administration of elections is within the governing scope of the individual states. But a federal system in which states all differ and in an era following extensive devolution of policy from the federal level to the state level, the decisions regarding what to do about reforming the electoral process is no easy task.

According to one recent study of the status of states and their compliance with the HAVA, there are currently no states that are in complete compliance with all of the provisions of the HAVA (The Constitution Project – http://www.electionline.org/site/dav/pdf/eripbrief32003.pdf). In fact, there are an estimated 35 states that fail to meet any of its requirements as of this writing.

Another key provision of the HAVA is the establishment of an Election Assistance Commission to:

> serve as a national clearinghouse and resource for the compilation of information and review of procedures with respect to the administration of Federal elections (Pub. L. 107-252).

At the present time, the Federal Election Commission is the national level authority that has the most oversight of the electoral system and the extent of that oversight authority is, to say the least, very limited in scope. Established in 1975, that organization is concerned only with enforcing the Federal Election Campaign Act - the statute that governs the financing of federal elections. It has no authority to oversee the operations of elections, per se. Therefore, although they do maintain some information, such as voter registration statistics as reported by the states, election returns for federal offices, and basic background information on the type and nature of voting equipment used across the country, their primary focus is on the financial aspect of political campaigns in the U.S. As a result, until the passage of the HAVA, there was no one source that citizens and researchers could turn to for obtaining information on elections. If this organization is established carefully in accordance with the provisions of the HAVA, it will set voluntary minimum standards for state election authorities to follow. This could result in a more standardized process, to a degree, of elections as conducted across the individual states. However, since these standards will be voluntary, again, it will be up to the wisdom and discretion of decision-makers within each state to implement these standards to their best advantage. Ultimately, though, there are no guarantees that it will result in a standardized process, at all. Again, much of this will depend on whether states choose to apply for funds made available through this Commission. If they take the money, they must live up to the voluntary standards. They trade-off their discretionary authority over the voluntary standards to obtain federal dollars.

A Little For Everyone

The various provisions of the HAVA listed in this chapter are all attempts within the framework of the incremental process to alter the electoral system and make it one that is more palatable to the majority of citizens and special interest groups in the United States. Each player in the arena impacted, in some way, on the measure produced. Perhaps, poet Alfred Lord Tennyson's words, "I am a part of all I have met" are most applicable to the HAVA, since it reflects the desires and preferences of a majority of the players in the arena, even though it fails to meet the optimal level of satisfaction of any one of those individual players.

What the actual HAVA produces will, ultimately, be dependent upon the policy implementation process. That implementation will form the working reality of the electoral process once election administrators begin to work with the newly enacted law. There were, in effect, three objectives that decision-makers had in mind when they crafted this law. They attempted to improve the existing electoral system; to satisfy the concerns of a diverse special interest audience and general citizenry; and, to take themselves off the hook when, at some future date, unintended consequences begin to appear.

The electoral process in America post-HAVA will, likely, change the contours of that process, but only by degrees. It is a measure that will cost the taxpayers dearly without providing the substantial equal protection of the vote that was part of the marketing strategy for passage of the bill. It is also one, though, that shifts any potential backlash by a disgruntled citizenry off of the backs of Congress and onto those of state legislators and election administrators, as noted earlier in this chapter. Who will it be, that ultimately stands accountable when, at some distant point in the future, the unintended consequences of this reform measure begin to surface and what will the actions taken to alleviate those consequences be?

Conclusion

This chapter argued that at this point in time several factors are working against systemic electoral reform. Although we have a reform measure that is bipartisan in nature and hailed as the solution to voting problems, the outcome is far from certain. The current measure, the HAVA, presented to the American people as sweeping reform, is essentially an incremental approach developed as a negotiated compromise between the interested parties.

In the next chapter, we will examine some of the potential trouble spots and shortcomings of the reform measure passed by Congress in October of 2002. Additionally, a discussion will be undertaken into the nature of public policymaking and its implications for the reform of the voting process in the United States.

Notes

[i] "Speaker Hastert Declares Passage of Election Reform Bill A Great Victory." Speaker.gov Newsroom, October 10, 2002, available online at: http://www.speaker.gov/library/agenda/021010elect.asp.
[ii] Available online at http://www.ncsl.org/programs/legman/elect/taskfc/TackleElectRef.htm.
[iii] Help America Vote Act of 2002. Pub. L. 107-252, Oct. 29, 2002. 116 Stat. 1666.
[iv] See remarks of Stephen Ansolabehere before the U.S. House Committee on Science, May 22, 2001.
[v] Testimony of Stephen Knack before the U.S. Senate Committee on Rules and Administration, March 14, 2001.
[vi] National Conference of State Legislatures. 2002. "Electoral Reform Across the States." Available online at www.ncsl.org.
[vii] Testimony by Larry J. Sabato, Director of the University of Virginia Center for Governmental Studies, before the U.S. Senate Committee on Rules and Administration, June 27, 2001.
[viii] Press release by the Lawyers' Committee for Civil Rights Under Law distributed on November 17, 2000.
[ix] Testimony before the U.S. Senate Committee on Rules and Administration of Deborah M. Phillips, Chairman of The Voting Integrity Project, March 14, 2001.

Chapter Five
Cosmetic Fix For A Systemic Problem

> *"Even when laws have been written down, they ought not always to remain unaltered."*
> – Aristotle (322 B.C.)

Prognosis For Success

In the 1960s, former President Lyndon Johnson set about ridding the country of poverty through an elaborate system of social welfare policies known as the Great Society programs in what was termed his *War On Poverty*. While those policies restructured the way in which wealth in America was redistributed and even alleviated some of the burdens associated with poverty, at that time, the Great Society programs did not eliminate the country's pockets of poverty as policymakers had envisioned.

Similarly, the voting reform measure was presented to the American people as sweeping change and as an end to problems of equal protection of the individual vote. This chapter will engage in a discussion of some of the inadequacies of the reform measure in the world of practical electoral activity that prevent the measure from living up to the image of it portrayed by its sponsors and congressional leadership. The myth of achieving a perfect electoral system through the current vision of reform will be discussed.

Throughout the preceding four chapters, I have repeatedly raised the issue of the ephemeral nature of reform, in general, and election reform, in particular. While in the abstract it might seem plausible, can one measure satisfy the concerns of all parties to the problem in the real world? Perhaps, our expectation of what we call reform is unrealistic. Will individuals and/or groups that pushed for reform be satisfied with the provisions of the Help America Vote Act (HAVA) when it becomes apparent to them that it is a symbolic measure? If there is inadequate enforcement of the existing Americans With Disabilities Act, for instance, will a newly created Election Assistance Commission be able to step up that enforcement? The answer is, it depends, among other things, on where you happen to reside.

Federal programs are not applied uniformly across the country. Rather, they vary according to the priority given them from one locality to another (Thomas, 1979). The effectiveness of federal programs, which the Elections Assistance Commission would become, in effect, will depend upon the degree of consideration that each election jurisdiction accords it. Regulatory enforcement is, at best, accomplished in a sporadic fashion. Regardless of the amount of resources allocated to accomplish that enforcement, traditionally it is never enough.

A few examples of where the individual states are, today, with regard to compliance with several of the provisions contained in the HAVA will help to exemplify this. The HAVA requires states to comply with several provisions pertaining to provisional voting, enabling individuals who believe they are registered to vote to be able to do so without facing undue hardship when they arrive at the polls. As of this writing, many of the states are struggling to meet compliance.

Similarly, although there are a few states that currently comply with the provisions of the HAVA that mandate a statewide voter registration database within each state, and another few are close to being in complete compliance, the vast majority are not.

Experience demonstrates, and literature supports, that the political climate of the individual states, a constantly changing condition, is a significant contributor to the decisions made by both federal and local officials (Hedge and Scicchitano, 1994). High priority today does not guarantee high priority tomorrow. If the political climate shifts, so do the policy preferences. The fact that there is a good deal of discord in the information arena surrounding the adequacy of the HAVA as a viable electoral reform measure, probably makes this an even more significant point. Conflict present at the beginning of the implementation stage may create a rocky foundation that will eventually cave in under continuous pressure.

The U.S. Supreme Court in *Bush v. Gore* found that the Florida recount process had created an equal protection problem with regard to a voter's rights. This was based, primarily, on the absence of any standards as to what constituted a spoiled ballot:

> The petition presents the following questions: whether the Florida Supreme Court established new standards for resolving Presidential election contests, thereby violating Art. II, § 1, cl. 2, of the United States Constitution and failing to comply with 3 U.S.C. § 5, and whether the use of standardless manual recounts violates the Equal Protection and Due Process Clauses. With respect to the equal protection question, we find a violation of the Equal Protection Clause.(p.1)

It wasn't the voting equipment that took center stage in the Court's focus of voting problems, but the standards used to judge the outputs of the voting machinery, instead. The HAVA attempts to create a degree of uniformity across the states by creating a set of standards that each state must comply with.

Although some of the problems associated with voting equipment in the provisions of the HAVA were detailed in the preceding chapter, some additional points need to be addressed at this juncture in order to place the matter of voting problems and reform into a broader context. Members of the Supreme Court were aware that any decision they made would be insufficient to resolve matters and, in fact, would act as a catalyst for future actions on behalf of the states.

On the surface, it seems plausible to accept the argument that punch card systems must be replaced with newer, better performing equipment. After all, if the older machines are more error-prone, why not replace them? Given that money has been made available to the states, albeit, in the form of matching grants, for this purpose, it would seem to be the logical course of action. In fact, the Supreme Court in *Bush v. Gore* took it for granted that the states would be considering such a move:

> This case has shown that punch card balloting machines can produce an unfortunate number of ballots which are not punched in a clean, complete way by the voter. After the current counting, it is likely legislative bodies nationwide will examine ways to improve the mechanisms and machinery for voting. (p.2)

The members of the Supreme Court who stood in the majority were no less guilty of falling victim to this short-term thinking than anyone else in society might be. Taking a forced look down the road into the not too distant future, though, presents a very different scenario. It becomes apparent that what will happen is an endless technology chase to keep one step ahead of the very problems of equal protection that the Court tried to prevent in the first place.

As technological advances to voting equipment are made and newer, more efficient products are developed, those jurisdictions that can afford to replace what is considered today to be state-of-the-art equipment, but that becomes antiquated tomorrow will, if history is any indication, probably do so. The move to a newer voting system by one jurisdiction would place the voters in other jurisdictions in a precarious position with respect to equal protection of their votes. In those jurisdictions that cannot afford to replace existing equipment, or whose administrators see no need to replace it for whatever reason, would be in the very same position as those voters who claimed their vote is not equally protected by election authorities that allow punch card voting in their jurisdictions in 2000. In other words, there will be continual equal protection problems in this country as long as technology continues to advance. This is a distinct likelihood given the rapid advance in technology over the past several decades and as long as we, as a society, refuse to believe that it is people who build and operate that technology and people make mistakes.

The move toward seeking newer voting technology is already taking shape in the engineering arena. The current state-of-the-art equipment is the direct record electronic (DRE) voting equipment, a type of equipment that offers voters a user-friendly computerized voting means, but one which many consider to be inherently problematic based on the equipment's lack of voter-verified audit trail. In Election 2000, approximately 12.3% of the registered voters in the United States were in voting jurisdictions that had this particular type of equipment. That figure was up 5.6% from the figure of 7.7% reported by the Federal Election Commission (FEC) for the 1996 general election, their most recent figure.[i] It is a voting technology that is increasing in popularity across the country. Some experts, though, consider it to be one of the most troubling advances in voting technology, yet.

Rebecca Mercuri, Ph.D., an engineering professor at Bryn Mawr University who studies election voting technology and president of Notable Software, Inc., a computer engineering and software consulting company, has issued a national plea to all United States citizens to actively lobby decision-makers against making this type of equipment the standard across the country (http://www.notablesoftware.com). She points out that some of these machines have failed to live up to expectations in their usage and have been responsible for mis-recorded, as well as lost votes, in past elections.

At the present time, the DRE lacks a paper trail and that makes this equipment, Mercuri argues, particularly problematic. Her argument is a logical one. It is easy to see how an unchecked computer program might become a potential ticket to vote fraud. An unethical and/or unscrupulous computer programmer could, conceivably, become a prime instrument by which election fraud could occur and there would be no way to identify the misdeed and/or to rectify it. A paper trail is an audit trail. It gives us a sense of security knowing that we can retrace our steps. In a society that values open government and provides citizens the right to access the information of government through an assortment of freedom of information laws at both the national and state levels, a voting system that leaves no trail fails to conform to the existing culture. Culture, in its political variety, is an important contributor to the choice of voting equipment employed across the states (Fife and Miller, 2002). There is no reason to believe that it will cease to play a role in the future choices made with regard to the voting equipment, as well.

Suggestions for other types of voting systems have been made over the past several years. Internet voting, for instance, has been suggested as a viable voting technology, would be practically feasible for deployment in the very near future, and could increase voter turnout. The convenience of being able to vote for political candidates from one's home cannot be disputed. Still, not everyone in American society owns a home computer. Early evidence from studies on I-voting (I-voting) suggests that the affluent in society might benefit more than the poor (Gibson, 2001/2002).

At the very least, remote locations such as traditional polling places or specially designated locations, such as voter kiosks, would still be needed to provide computer terminals for those who could not avail themselves of their right to vote through their own means. The remote locations would produce their own set of problems. Persons with disabilities would still require accommodations to assist them in voting, in some cases, and provisions would have to be made for citizens with English language limitations. One need only take the example of the confusion produced by self-ticketing kiosks in airports when they were introduced to understand this. People required a good deal of assistance to figure out how to use them.

It would take time for state and local election administrators to work out the details of implementing this type of voting system. The infrastructure is not in place at the current time for such a system to be easily implemented. During the interim period of I-voting phase-in, there would be pockets of equal protection violations as some voting jurisdictions adopt it while others struggle to catch up. Additionally, the HAVA provides a one-time appropriation of funds. There are no provisions for future problems of equal protection potentially caused by voting equipment technology changes. The HAVA would also have to be amended at some point because I-voting was not one of the five currently employed voting systems considered in the deliberations over the HAVA and, therefore, it was not considered when the monies were appropriated. It would involve a new wave of appropriations at some future date to help states pay for the upgrade. Given that appropriations are not easily gotten out of Congress by the states, this undoubtedly would involve a lengthy campaign by the states to secure the monies necessary for that upgrade.

Another potential problem with I-voting involves the security of each person's vote. According to a National Science Foundation press release dated March 6, 2001,

> Remote voting holds the greatest promise of convenience and universal access, but it also poses substantial security issues in addition to other risks. E-voting requires a much greater level of security than e-commerce...
> (NSF–http://www.nsf.gov/od/lpa/news/press/01/pr0118.htm).

The security of an individual's personal vote would be difficult, at best, to adequately police. Computers are hacked into every day in both the public and private domains. The government is increasingly issuing warnings about the havoc that could result from massive computer hacking and its disruption of Internet traffic. Given this, it would only be a matter of time before hackers discovered how to steal an individual's vote. Tracking this type of crime down to its source would be an arduous, if not impossible, task.

Integrating new technologies into the voting process is only one of many potential problems. Other aspects of the electoral process are inherently problematic, as well. Changes mandated by the HAVA regarding voter registration databases across the states will alleviate some of the inaccuracies in the existing lists, but it cannot guarantee that all individuals will have an equal chance of freely participating in the voting process unhampered by errors in the databases. As noted in the preceding chapter, even before the HAVA became law, there were those who understood that while changes in voter status in the cases of voters who move from one voting jurisdiction within a state to another would be easier to track, the HAVA, as it is written, does nothing to alleviate problems of interstate jurisdictional changes. At some point in the future, the databases across the states would have to be interfaced to accommodate voters who move from one state to another, but that would not be an easy task given that it would require a nationalization of the election process, a measure not likely to happen anytime soon.

The HAVA mandated the creation of a foundation that will grant funds for research into improving the electoral process, whether that involves voting equipment, voter education, or worker training. This newly created entity will open the door to a new understanding of the complexities involved in the election process and its inherent difficulties that may lead to different ways of conducting elections in the future. The reform will breed its own continual reform, in essence. As more is learned, expectations of the system will change. The forces of time cannot be stopped. Neither can the changes brought about by that passage of time.

The public policy process is a complex one that has garnered a good deal of attention by scholars over the past several decades. Throughout the previous chapters, I have attempted to make clear the multiplicity of participants and perspectives that have contributed to the creation of the HAVA, billed by its sponsors and congressional leadership as a sweeping reform measure. Pressman and Wildavsky (1973) have noted that this multiplicity of participants and perspectives have contributed in a variety of public policy areas to the difficulties associated with implementing public programs.

Majone and Wildavsky (1995) point out that implementation of public policy begins with this multiplicity in terms of the actions of the participants in that they continuously work toward shaping those policies according to the goals of the participants. Policy is, therefore, a continuously evolving process that has no end.

If one accepts this premise, and I do, then the idea that public policies are "reformed" becomes problematic. If policies are constantly evolving, they are constantly reforming. But, reform is not simply policy evolution; it is distinctly different from ordinary day-to-day policy evolution in tactical terms.

Lipsky (1982) argued that public policy becomes what it is interpreted to be by those who must enforce the policy on a daily basis. The police officers who must give traffic tickets decide on a case-by-case basis how to issue those tickets; the firefighters who rush into the burning buildings make decisions of what is appropriate usage of policy in each case, and so on. These folks, the workers, do not consciously reform the policies, per se, but they do contribute to the evolution of those policies as their interaction with citizens develops their expectations based on the behaviors that they witness among those workers with whom they interact. We come to expect what we are conditioned to on a daily basis.

Organizational behavior scholars evidence self-esteem needs as an important part of employee productivity. Individuals are motivated to perform well in the workplace by their own need to feel good about themselves. Lipsky (1982) points out that public employees try to perform their jobs effectively even though they see themselves as performing those tasks under a serious set of constraints, and they are likely to leave those jobs if they develop a recognition of their own work as being less than adequate. Under this scenario, it is unlikely that they engage in any strategic effort to change the policies they are given to carry out. They attempt to carry them out, but if they can't do that to their own satisfaction, they seek work elsewhere.

Reform involves something quite different from normal policy evolution. Reform involves a strategic change that forces the illusion of an extraordinary alteration of the policy provisions on those subject to the policies. It is a public call for a fundamental alteration of what exists. Reform begins with the goal of publicly transforming what is into what could be out in the arena in which the multiple perspectives will be generated. This is, quite different, therefore, from what scholars, particularly Majone and Wildavsky (1995), have depicted in the policy process. Where ordinary evolution of policy involves a continuous subtle transformation, reform is an overt transformation that is outside the ordinary course of normal daily activities. It begins with a specific and anticipated action on the part of some individual or group and is intended primarily to create change for some specific reason. It differs from normal policy evolution in this regard, particularly with respect to its strategic nature.

Every systems model of the policy process includes stages of implementation and evaluation of public policies. When the evaluation stage of the process produces evidence of substantial variation between what was intended and what exists, it becomes apparent to attentive audiences that the original policies need to be clarified and/or amended. In terms of election reform, specifically, the subject of this work, the events of Election 2000 were extraordinary enough in and of themselves to capture the attention of even those audiences that are routinely somewhat inattentive and, therefore, forced decision-makers into a position where they had to respond to conditions in the public arena where both citizens and special interest groups had begun deliberating reform on their own. They demanded of the decision-makers, in this case those sitting in Congress, some action that would force change. Multiple participants in society were not content to let the electoral policies of the United States take their normal evolutionary course, or at least that was the perception of key members of Congress. Those decision-makers responded to what they perceived to be a public outcry for change among individuals and groups that were attentive to the political process and, particularly, to their own role in altering policies that were counter to their own preferences or what they regarded as their own well-being.

The result of this perception was the series of bargains and deals struck in the congressional domain between participants over the reform-initiative as each of those participants demanded a platform for launching their own particular perspectives as solutions to the problems of voting. The HAVA is a policy measure crafted by the inputs of the multiple participants and their perspectives. The HAVA, as a policy, will now follow the same course through the implementation and evaluation stages of the public policy process as any other policy. In those stages, there will be participants who are not happy and who will seek to change, yet again, the policy as it exists in an attempt to gain an even greater amount of power in impacting the policy process. In other words, those who are dissatisfied with the electoral process after the HAVA will seek to amend it into something that more closely resembles their own perspective of how it should operate. They will become disenchanted with what they believed to be permanent and fundamental change.

Assigning Blame For Disappointment

What will happen when the participants to the reform process, or those who were inattentive to that process as it occurred, begin to become dissatisfied with the outcomes of that measure as implemented? The causal chain is too complex for the average citizen to take the time to analyze the components that went into the creation of the HAVA to be able to successfully identify the true cause of any unintended consequences that may develop as a result of its implementation. There will be no easy villain to blame for the conditions that fail to live up to their original vision, in the case of those who supported reform. While we do not have a crystal ball that will allow us to see the point in the future where this will occur, it is apparent that not all of the concerns that surfaced in the reform environment were accommodated. Even at this point, well in advance of the deadlines for compliance with the HAVA noted in Figure I, indications are clear that it will fail to live up to the dreams and expectations of all the players at the reform table. This, according to the conditions outlined in the first chapter, posits that this measure will only temporarily satisfy a sufficient number of people in the United States with regard to the way in which we conduct our elections to keep them operating under existing rules. We will need to reform again and again and again, as time, technology, and our own expectations change with changing conditions. This, after all, is to be expected given what we know of the incrementalist nature of policy-making in the United States.

Lindblom (1959) defined incrementalism as the best strategy for public policymaking currently known. Linblom's praise of incrementalism first appeared in a 1959 article in the *American Public Administration Review*. It has been reprinted a number of times and, having been advanced little by scholars since his work, Lindblom's theory stands as the premier work on incrementalism to date among public policy scholars. Lindblom highlights the limitations of radical public policymaking due to the constraints inherently a part of a pluralistic society and the limitations of comprehensive rational planning due to economic and cognitive constraints. In a sense, Lindblom's incrementalism advances Popper's notion of piecemeal social engineering written about in approximately the same time period.[ii] Popper believed that all empirically tested theory and subsequent scientifically generated knowledge was, by its nature, impossible to verify since it is inconceivable that the human mind could envision every possible alternative at one time, a feat which would be beyond human cognitive ability. Both Lindblom (1995) and Popper (1992/1959) provided us with evidence that supports a rational approach to policymaking within a set of constraints. It is, therefore, not surprising that changing the way America votes would be a difficult undertaking and that the initial policy efforts aimed at reforming the current system of voting would produce a set of unintended consequences at some future date. It is a condition to be expected. Popper's (1992/1959) writings should have prepared us for the inevitability of unintended consequences in all policy measures introduced in a changing public arena. Policy evolves because it never satisfies all of the people all of the time. When attentive audiences begin to become dissatisfied, the momentum toward change intensifies and reform is born. Yet, reform, like its counterpart, continuous normal policy evolution, is doomed from its inception because of the diverse set of self-interests held by the people who drift in and out of the arena as players in the system at varying times.

Electoral reform is like the old child's riddle, what comes and comes yet never gets here? Tomorrow, of course. We reform and reform again and again, yet we never seem to get it right. Perhaps, the answer to this stares us directly in

FIGURE I – HAVA Deadlines

Federal Standards and Requirement	Deadlines
Voting System Standards	January 1, 2006
Provisional Voting Requirements	January 1, 2004
Computerized Statewide Voter Registration List	January 1, 2004, with waiver to January 1, 2006
Anti-Fraud and Voter Identification Procedures	January 1, 2004, with waiver to January 1, 2006
Mail-in Registration Requirements	January 1, 2004

Source: National Governors' Association
Available online at: http://www.nga.org/nga/lobbyIssues/1,1169,D_4893,00.html.

the face, but we refuse to acknowledge it. We cannot find a "fix" to the problem because there is no one way to fix it. We live in a culture that supports the notion that we can take a pill at bedtime and wake up in the morning cured. In the case of public policy, there is no magic pill to be taken. As a society, we must accept the fact that because change is a constant, we must continuously monitor and maintain the public policies that we enact in response to those changes. The notion of reform is a term employed in political rhetoric by those who wish to take control of policy for specific purposes.

The United States Congress was the vehicle that delivered the reform measure that will change the way America votes. Congressional decision-makers were responsible for the initial policy that will create that change; they effectively shifted the burden of responsibility for that voting onto the individual states whose own decision-makers will, ultimately, have to decide the fate of voting within their own jurisdictions. Are any of these folks to blame for what will, undoubtedly, disappoint and frustrate some in the future? Perhaps, they are, but only to a degree. They acted prematurely when the best interests of the country would have been served by sitting back and waiting for more knowledge to surface. However, in another sense, they were constrained by their own limitations. Legislators at both the national and state levels are charged with carrying out the will of the people. The people, for the most part, failed to register in on this issue to any great extent. Legislators are not, in general, trained policy analysts and should not be expected to be. It is, though, their responsibility to not act hastily in carrying out their duties.

Conclusion

Having established the incrementalist nature of the reform measure presented to the American people, this chapter engaged in a discussion of the inadequacies of the reform measure in the world of practical electoral activity. The myth of achieving a perfect electoral system through the current vision of reform is discussed. What does the enactment of this new public policy regarding the way in which America votes mean in terms of the vitality of democracy? Will it have any long-term or fundamental effect on that democracy? The next chapter will engage in a discussion of the HAVA in terms of its impact on American democracy.

Notes

[i] That figure is available online from the Federal Election Commission. 2002b. About Elections and Voting. Available online at: http://www.fec.gov/pages/dre.htm.

[ii] Popper, Karl. 1992/1959. *The Logic of Scientific Discovery.* New York, NY: Routledge, Inc.

Chapter Six
Democracy And The Future Of Elections In America

> *"Democracy cannot succeed unless those who express
> their choice are prepared to choose wisely. The real
> safeguard of democracy, therefore, is education."*
> - Franklin Delano Roosevelt[i]

Policy Change: Evolution/Reform

It should come as no surprise to readers of this work that the process of electoral reform has taken place amid a series of bargaining and negotiations. The hallmark of the American democratic system has been its ability, with several notable exceptions, to encompass diverse groups of people into the public affairs arena. In one of the outstanding classics of political science, *A Preface to Democratic Theory,* Robert Dahl (1956) intrigued generations of political science scholars by arguing that the "American Hybrid" of polyarchal democracy functions by allowing the preferences of distinct minorities to be heard and to be effective in their pursuit of their policy preferences even in the face of distinct opposition from the majority. Dahl argues that it is precisely because of this ability to become a part of and to impact on the public policy process that democracy works. Although inherently a messy process, it allows for a venting of the discontentment with policy specifics and, therefore, for a continuous and dynamic shifting of the resources across society. Dahl sums it up as follows:

> It is not a static system. The normal American system has evolved, and by evolving it has survived...so long as the social prerequisites of democracy are substantially intact in this country, it appears to be a relatively efficient system for reinforcing agreement, encouraging moderation, and maintaining social peace in a restless

and immoderate people operating a gigantic, powerful, diversified, and incredibly complex society.

This evolution of policy and its impact on the shift of resources is not unidimensional in nature. It has a multidimensional influence across democracy because it occurs within a multidimensional and dynamic environment. As change is brought about in the particulars of specific policies, the policies contribute to their own evolution as they continue to alter the expectations of society so that there is never a return to what was known, but a continual march into new uncharted territory. The bar gets raised for successive iterations of policy changes so that our definition of equality becomes ever more finely tuned. The specific changes brought about by electoral reform will take on a form that is characterized by the specific influences placed on them in the implementation stage.

Some of the mandates of the Help America Vote Act (HAVA) will be carried out as envisioned by the decision-makers; others will be carried out as interpreted by those who must implement them on a daily basis. The true impact of the reform measure, though, will be found in its ability to alter the expectations of the majority of citizens as to what constitutes the meaning of equal protection of the vote in the United States as they attempt to participate in the public affairs process by attempting to cast their individual votes. If their expectations do not match up with the reality of what they encounter, proponents of the reform will believe the measure will have failed them. At that point, a new move toward yet another reform will begin to gel.

Most certainly, the ideal voting process, as envisioned by those reformers, both among the citizenry and the body of institutional decision-makers, will fail to become a reality. As indicated in the previous chapter, there are already trouble spots with election reform that have become apparent. The failure of reformers to accomplish the creation of a nationally linked voter registration database on a specific level and the inability of federal administrators to adequately enforce existing laws such as the Voting Rights and Americans With Disabilities Acts, on a broader level, are examples of problems that the reform did not alleviate, but that will have to be addressed at some point in the future. The reform measure, aka the HAVA, is a cosmetic fix to what is a systemic problem bred from human nature.

In the real world of public affairs, there is no perfection nor should our expectations lead us to believe there is. Yet, democracy in the United States rests on a set of ideals that includes equality. Without it, self-governance as we have come to know it makes no sense. We must strive to achieve equality if our way of life is to continue.

At the same time, while the ideal is something we should strive for, we must also be realistic in our understanding that we can never achieve it. Equal protection of the vote is an ideal that we should strive for, but we should also be cognizant of the fact that there can never be total protection of equality for a variety of reasons, not the least of which is that as rational self-interested creatures, we seek the lions' share of resources for ourselves and worry about redistributing those resources only secondarily.

It is an unfortunate artifact of self-interested human nature that there will always be a struggle in society between the haves, or those who hold the resources, and the have-nots who want to hold more of them. Alexander Hamilton characterized this societal struggle for resources in theoretical terms when he said:

> Give all power to the many, they will oppress the few. Give all power to the few, they will oppress the many. Both therefore ought to have power, that each may defend itself agst. the other. (http://www.constitution.org/dfc/dfc_0618.htm)

Public policy in the best interests of all is that which strikes a balance among all of those interests. In this sense, the litmus test for the success of the HAVA as a strategic alteration of the electoral process will be the amount of time it takes for dissatisfaction to begin to re-appear across the citizenry and special interest groups who were and continue to be attentive to these matters. The problems of voting in the United States have not been wiped away; they are bound to return at some point. Obviously, in the absence of a crystal ball, how far down the road that point is becomes a question we have no answer for.

Although at times throughout this work it would appear that I have preached gloom and doom, this analysis is not meant to lead the reader down a pessimistic path that fails to produce anything constructive. To the contrary, it is meant to inspire the search for a way to fine-tune the public policy process so that unintended consequences can be reduced in the quest to find a way for all citizens to participate freely and unencumbered in the public affairs arena. Pointing out the pitfalls of attempts by individuals and groups to change the primary vehicle that delivers that self-government, the voting system, need not detract from efforts to enhance the system, but rather to begin to chart a course of future action based on knowledge acquired at this point.

Understanding that reform is a strategically manipulated set of actions, being cognizant that it is a political theater of sorts, gives us the ability to recognize signs that may begin to appear that the intense preferences that often lead to the demand for reform are building. Dahl (1956) argued that an accurate estimation of the intensities of preferences allows decision-makers to design rules aimed at stabilizing democracy. Accurate estimation of the intensities coupled with an in-depth understanding of whether the preferences of minorities are, in fact, based on knowledge sufficient to provide a strong probability of being able to resolve a problem is necessary for decision-makers to use as a guide in determining when the appropriate time is to take decisive action to invite public input on reform measures. In other words, a more systematic approach is needed to prevent the premature creation and enactment of public policies that could have severe unintended consequences. Policymakers need to be sensitive to the impact

97

of their actions on the health and vitality of democracy rather than simply to their own political expediency.

As human beings, we are limited creatures. Although our knowledge base is rapidly expanding, it is only a fraction of what there is to know in the world. An action that appears to be an alternative that we believe is in our best interest often turns out in retrospect to be the very worst alternative that we could have chosen. Alternatives preferred by minorities in a democracy are often courses of action that elevate short-term power standing at the expense of their long-term well-being. Public policies need to be carefully analyzed prior to adoption in order to avoid as many of these situations as possible, recognizing that we can't, of course, avoid all of them. Critics may argue that it is striving for perfection, but it is only in striving for perfection that we may find the added incentive to forge ahead.

An example of a reform measure that satisfied immediate short-term concerns at the expense of long-term gains of minority groups can be found in the case of the demise of cumulative voting, a proportional form of representation, in the Illinois legislature. In 1980, a movement in Illinois led by a small group of reformers introduced the idea of reducing the size of that legislature in order to keep the rising costs of running the legislative process down. A successful grassroots campaign to promote a binding voter referendum to reduce the size of the legislature by one-third ultimately was voted in by the citizens who had been angered by a recent tax increase. A decade later, though, the cutback was criticized as a move that jeopardized the chances of women and minority populations for gaining access to elected office by making it more difficult to unseat incumbents.[ii] The smaller size of the House of Representatives resulted in a new set of problems. Yet, a simple lesson in Illinois history might have indicated the potential of that reform measure to produce unintended consequences.

Cumulative voting was introduced to Illinois as a reform measure of its own back in 1870. It was a "home-grown system of minority representation" by policy advocate Joseph Medill, then owner of the *Chicago Tribune*, who proposed the system as a means to help heal a sectional split between legislators from the northern and southern parts of the state.[iii] In essence, voters could cast a single vote for each of three candidates, one and a half votes for two candidates, or three votes for a single candidate. Under this system, the minority party in each district was able to elect at least one voice to represent it in the statehouse. Without it, the dominant party wins the election and is the only voice representing the entire district, the problematic condition that existed prior to the original policy reform.

A little over a century later, reformers rid the state of the cumulative voting system. Although instituted as a cost-savings measure, unintended consequences quickly followed as, according to Wheeler:

> ...the switch to single-member House districts has seen troubling developments: a concentration of legislative power in party leaders, less independence among the membership, fewer votes cast on principle rather than on politics, and increasing regional polarization of the two parties...[iv]

It is apparent that, according to its opponents and to some political science scholars, this measure did little to foster democracy in the governance of public affairs in Illinois.[v] What succeeded as a popular move to reform a public policy created an even greater problem for the underlying vitality of self-governance. As the old adage goes, "he who does not learn from history is doomed to repeat it." Failure to learn our lessons from American history will do little to nurture the democratic process across the United States. Like gerbils on a wheel, successive generations of citizens will continue to repeat past mistakes, wasting precious time and energy that could be better spent in devising and exploring new alternatives.

Opportunity Created

The HAVA may just have provided a means for potentially channeling activity along the route to the exploration of new alternatives through two of its specific provisions. American political scholars have long known that education plays a crucial role in the political socialization process (Almond and Verba, 1965). More recent evidence suggests that education makes a difference in the knowledge levels of American citizens and that knowledgeable citizens are the ones most likely to acquire new information (Delli Carpini and Keeter, 1996). The more education citizens receive, therefore, greater the knowledge they carry around with them and the more likely they are to gain even greater amounts of knowledge over time. With the provision of the HAVA that requires performance of and provides funds for research studies into both current and alternate methods of a variety of aspects of the voting system as it exists across the states, the potential exists for unprecedented discoveries of avenues for enhancing this particular and most common form of participation in the democratic process.[vi]

Election scholars, while traditionally tapping into one of the more popular avenues of research, have been given a tremendous incentive for pursuing their areas of interest that will, most likely, attract additional scholars to this line of inquiry. The dialogue among this growing group of scholars will generate a wider range of ideas that can only benefit the democratic process. The more ideas there are, the greater the chance for discovery of improved methods of voting. Now that change has become a reality – however, extensive or limited it may be in nature - the opportunity presents itself to advance scientific knowledge regarding our ways of voting by engaging in what Popper (1959/1992) referred to as the path of science through rigorous testing and corroborability of the theories that we, as a society, operate under. While we have come a long way from the time of Popper, his vision of science is still very much rooted in the methods of analysis that are a central part of the rational, or more precisely its offshoot, the incrementalist, paradigm. As such, we have a starting point from which to begin testing the policies codified in the HAVA as they are implemented and commence the evolutionary process that is a part of all public policy. Once this occurs, the real work begins. The actual work that went into enactment of the HAVA was only the prelude to the work yet to come as we seek to capitalize on the HAVA as a tool for cultivating our democratic form of government.

We cannot enhance democracy without subjecting our assumptions about the methods with which we operate it to close scrutiny. We cannot fool ourselves into believing that we have achieved perfection for, at best, we can only approximate what we believe to be perfection based on the constraints that limit our potential. We also cannot assume that reform necessarily places us in a better position, since the unintended consequences may turn out to be worse than the original problems. Additional research into the nature and process of our voting systems will pay rich dividends in the amounts of knowledge available to voters and practitioners. Additional research will result in the advancement of the knowledge that generates theories because it is only through systematic inquiry that we advance our knowledge. This provision will allow members of the policy analysis community to forge ahead in their work of testing and retesting the theories that form the foundation of the HAVA and its link to democracy. In the spirit of Popper, this is a necessary part of the public policy process.

The second provision that stands to be of great value in enhancing the voting process and, therefore, the democratic process, is that which provides funding to encourage greater student participation in the electoral arena as nonpartisan poll workers and for projects designed to stimulate participatory activity among the younger generation. College-level students will be targeted for integration into the electoral process through a newly created "Help America Vote Program" and high school students through projects of this type funded through the "Help America Vote Foundation."[vii] These programs are efforts designed around the concept of service-learning experiences in one of the first programs of its kind institutional directives with the ultimate goal of participation in mind.

Hopefully, these initiatives will inspire younger minds to seek out the types of information that will better prepare them for choosing among the often complex and vast array of alternatives that characterize the sets of policy decisions to be made. These programs, together with knowledge garnered from additional research will form the foundation for the future of enhanced voting policy. Helping today's students to think critically through the alternatives that they will encounter in designing and implementing public policy; for students to be able to distinguish fact from fiction, reality from idealism, and so on will produce rich results as they advance into tomorrow's citizens prepared to take over the reins of decision-making. One thing is certain; they cannot be expected to make sound decisions in the absence of exposure to pertinent information.[viii] Exposing students to political experience opens up their minds to the possibility of accepting new information, thereby providing a firmer foundation for future decision-making in their undertakings.

Ultimately, the particular types of voting equipment employed, the placement of that equipment, and so on should be viewed as of secondary importance to that of the search for more productive and efficient means of accomplishing our goals, namely, to find ways to allow greater numbers of citizens to freely and wisely cast their votes. We become too embroiled in the political battles over today's resources and lose sight of our investment into tomorrow.

It is easy to forget that in a federal system, there are multiple political cultures operating at any given time that contribute to a varied set of preferences that often conflict with one another. The one-size-fits-all approach to administering elections mandated onto the states by the federal government fails to take this into account. The key to the future of enhanced democracy is to take advantage of those differences instead of seeing them as obstacles in a competition between future winners and losers. That can only be accomplished if we train ourselves to see the benefit in using our pooled resources as collateral to be invested toward preserving democracy in America.

The constant shift in the public opinion of citizens across the United States is healthy for the country as a whole because it serves to protect both the minority from being tyrannized by the majority and vice versa. It serves to check the power of the "haves" from imposing their will on the have-nots in society. Above all else, it serves as a foundation from which knowledge is generated as we live out the evolution of our public policies, whether that evolution comes about in the form of daily erosion or strategic interception. It exists in both the national and state levels of government and plays out in each decision made in the public affairs arena. Without it, the wheels that keep the machinery moving would cease their motion, and democracy, both as we know it and as we would like to see it in the future, would have been a failed experiment.

Notes

[i] Franklin D. Roosevelt. 1982. In Beilenson, Peter and Helen Beilenson (eds): *The Wit and Wisdom of Franklin D. Roosevelt, Government and Democracy.* White Plains, NY: Peter Pauper Press, p. 29.
[ii] The Web site for the Midwest Democracy Center's Illinois Citizens for Proportional Representation Project contains links to a variety of articles that argue for proportional representation as a system favorable to democratic societies including Hill, Steven and Rob Richie. 2000. "Politicians Even Shake Down Their Own." *Christian Science Monitor.* 92(159): p.11.
[iii] See Wheeler III, Charles N. 1995. "Cure Sectionalism By Returning to Cumulative Voting System." *Illinois Municipal Review*, p. 13.
[iv] Ibid.
[v] Charles N. Wheeler III is a former Chicago *Sun-Times* reporter, and current director of the Public Affairs Reporting Program at the University of Illinois at Springfield.
[vi] See Appendix Onefor a complete list of the types of voting-related studies eligible for funding.
[vii] See Appendix One for a complete list of the types of voting-related studies eligible for funding.
[viii] While political sophistication is a controversial topic, whether individuals rely on facts or evaluations for political judgements, they must be exposed to information in the first place in order to make a decision. Whether the human mind then goes on to retain the fact or simply forms an evaluation based on forgotten facts becomes irrelevant.

APPENDICES

Appendix One

Pertinent Information on the Help America Vote Act
from the Congressional Research Service[i]

Congressional Documents

Congressional Black Caucus
Held hearings on election reform on February 27 and April 3, 2001.

U.S. House, Committee on Armed Services
On May 9, 2001, the Military Personnel Subcommittee held hearings on military voting. In this chronological listing of transcripts, select the highlighted sections of the May 9 Military Personnel Subcommittee entry for the opening statements of Chairman McHugh and of witnesses who submitted testimony electronically.

U.S. House, Committee on Government Reform, Minority
The minority staff of the Special Investigation Division of the Committee released a report on the effects of election reform efforts in Detroit in April 2001, and one on the effects of income and racial disparities in the 2000 presidential election in July 2001.

U.S. House, Committee on House Administration
This listing of Committee business includes agendas and transcripts from several hearings that the Committee held on election reform. The Committee reported H.R. 3295 (H. Rept., 107-329) on 10 December 2001. The House passed an amended version (see H. Rept., 107-331) on December 12.

U.S. House, Committee on the Judiciary
On December 5, 2001, the Committee held a hearing on H.R. 3295. The Committee's Democratic Investigative Staff released a report on problems in the 2000 election on August 20, 2001.

U.S. House, Committee on Science
Hearings were held on May 22, 2001, on the role of standards in improving voting technology. The Committee reported H.R. 2275 (H. Rept., 107-263) on October 31, 2001.

U.S. House, Democratic Caucus, Special Committee on Election Reform, Special Report
"Revitalizing Our Nation's Election System" was released in November 2001.

U.S. Senate, Committee on Commerce
Hearings on election reform were held March 7, 2001.

U.S. Senate, Committee on Governmental Affairs
Hearings, federal election practices and procedures were held on May 3 and May 9, 2001.

U.S. Senate, Committee on Rules and Administration
Hearings on election reform were held on March 14, June 27-28, and July 23, 2001.

See also the following pages in this briefing book: Congressional Bills, Floor Debate on S. 565, and Amendments to S. 565.

Data, Studies, and Reports

Advancement Project

The Advancement Project's report, "America's Modern Poll Tax: How Structural Disenfranchisement Erodes Democracy," released November 7, 2001, includes findings from the Project's survey of 43 election officials and makes seven recommendations, such as provisional voting.

Caltech/MIT

The Voting Technology Project, a joint effort of the California Technical Institute (Caltech) and Massachusetts Institute of Technology (MIT) is evaluating U.S. voting systems and establishing guidelines for performance and reliability. The Project's study, "Voting – What Is, What Could Be," was released July 16, 2001.

Cato Institute

Policy Analysis, number 417, October 23, 2001, presented "Election Reform, Federalism, and the Obligation of Voters."

Collins Center for Public Policy

Florida's The Governor's Select Task Force on Election Procedures, Standards, and Technology released its final report, "Revitalizing Democracy in Florida" on March 1, 2001.

Common Cause

"Not Making the Grade: A Year After Florida, Little Action in States on Election Reform" was published by the Common Cause Education Fund, which calls the report an election reform report card. The report is based on surveys of how the states measured up regarding four of the recommendations of the National Commission on Federal Election Reform (Carter-Ford Commission) that Common Cause endorses.

Constitution Project

The Forum on Election Reform was formed in February 2001 by the Constitution Project, and released its report, "Building Consensus on Election Reform," on August 2, 2001.

Election Center

The National Task Force on Election Reform findings, entitled "Election 2000: Review and Recommendations by the Nation's Elections Administrators," were published July 9, 2001.

Election Reform Information Project

The group published a report in October 2001, entitled "What's Changed, What Hasn't, and Why: Election Reform Since November 2000," that reviews developments in election reform over the last year.

Federal Voting Assistance Program (FVAP)

The FVAP and state and local officials conducted the Voting Over the Internet Pilot Project. An assessment report was issued in June 2001.

General Accounting Office's Election Reports

Elections: A Framework for Evaluating Reform Proposals. GAO-02-90, October 15, 2001.

Elections: Issues Affecting Military and Overseas Absentee Voters. GAO-01-704T, May 9, 2001.

Elections: Perspectives on Activities and Challenges Across the Nation. GAO-02-3, October 15, 2001.

Elections: Status and Use of Federal Voting Equipment Standards. GAO-02-52, October 15, 2001.

Elections: Voting Assistance to Military and Overseas Citizens Should Be Improved. GAO-01-1026, September 28, 2001.

Elections: The Scope of Congressional Authority to Polling Places and Alternative Voting Methods. GAO-02-107, October 15, 2001.

Voters with Disabilities: Access to Polling Places and Alternative Voting Methods. GAO-02-107, October 15, 2001.

George Washington University
The University's Institute for Communitarian Policy Studies issued this "Report on Election Reform Systems" in July 2001.

Georgia State Study
The Georgia Secretary of State issued this report on Georgia's registration and election systems on February 2, 2001. The report is entitled "The 2000 Election: A Wake-Up Call for Reform and Change."

HalfthePlanet.com's Voting Accessibility Department
This brief report contains survey results on voting rights of disabled persons. It is entitled "Voters Denied Equal Access at the Polls: A Report on the Status of Accessibility to Polling Places in the United States" and was done by the National Voter Independence Project.

Institute of Governmental Studies, University of California, Berkeley
The Survey Research Center and the Institute issued a joint report on the performance of voting technology in the United States in September 2001. The report is entitled "Counting All the Votes: The Performance of Voting Technology in the United States."

Maryland State Report and Recommendations
The Special Committee on Voting Systems and Election Procedures in Maryland issued its report in February 2001.

NACo/NACRC
The National Commission on Election Standards and Reform was formed by the National Association of County Recorders, Election Officials, and Clerks (NACRC) and National Association of Counties (NACo) to make recommendations for improvements in the nation's election system. The resulting "Report and Recommendations to Improve America's Election System" was issued in May 2001.

National Association of Secretaries of State (NASS)
NASS surveyed the states after the 2000 elections and summarized the results for this report. August 2001 is the latest update.

The National Commission on Federal Election Reform (Carter/Ford Commission)
The final report of the commission, "To Assure Pride and Confidence in the Electoral Process," released July 31, 2001, contains 13 major recommendations.

National Conference of State Legislatures (NCSL)
The Election Reform Task Force, consisting of 30 state legislators and legislative staff, made recommendations in 10 areas. The report is entitled "Voting in America: Final Report of the NCSL Elections Reform Task Force."

U.S. Commission on Civil Rights
The Commission released a report on "Voting Irregularities in Florida During the 2000 Presidential Election" in June 2001 and a report on "Election Reform: An Analysis of Proposals and the Commission's Recommendations for Improving America's Election Systems" in November 2001.

Federal Agencies

Federal Election Commission
The Commission's Office of Election Administration provides a wide range of election information including a draft update of the federal voting system standards.

Federal Voting Assistance Program
Official site for voting assistance to members of the military and to U.S. citizens living abroad.

General Accounting Office
A congressional support agency, the General Accounting Office published a number of evaluative reports in the year 2001 regarding election reform.

The Voting Section, Civil Rights Division
This Department of Justice office enforces federal voting rights laws. The Web page provides links to the major voting rights laws, such as the Uniform and Overseas Citizens Absentee Voting Act or the National Voter Registration Act, and includes further information on such laws.

U.S. Commission on Civil Rights

111

The Commission is an independent agency established under the Civil Rights Act to provide equal protection of laws, investigate charges of discrimination including the area of voting rights, and report to the President and Congress on its findings.

State and Local Government Organizations

The Council of State Governments (CSG)
A nonprofit, nonpartisan national organization, the Council's goal is to serve state officials and state governments, including providing information and research services.

National Association of Counties (NACo)
This national organization represents all the county governments in the United States. The group is active in legislative activities on behalf of county governments.

National Association of County Recorders, Election Officials, and Clerks (NACRC)
The professional organization of county administrative officials is the largest affiliate of the National Association of Counties (NACo). The Association's Web page provides information on election reform. The organization is active in legislative activities on the county government level.

National Association of Secretaries of State (NASS)
The Web site of this nonpartisan, professional organization of public officials offers links to all the Secretary of State pages and their election divisions. Provides white papers and reports from the states on election reform.

National Association of State Election Directors (NASED)

The Web site of this nonpartisan, professional organization of state election directors includes links to each state's election information. The Web page offers states' responses to legislative proposals for election reform.

National Conference of State Legislatures (NCSL)

The bipartisan organization's election reform legislation database enables searches by state and legislative action from a menu of subtopics.

Associations and Other Sites

Action Agenda for Electoral Reform

The *Nation* magazine, *Progressive Challenge*, and the Institute for Policy Studies cosponsor this election reform clearinghouse Web site. The site includes news articles, information on legislation, and issue briefs for a number of electoral reform issues, such as improving access to the ballot and the disenfranchisement of former felons.

Brookings Institution

The governmental studies section of the Brookings Institution Web site has an Election Reform Web page, which offers recent developments, current legislation, and related links; and an Internet Voting Web page. The site also makes available the Brookings Institution's policy briefing paper on election reform.

Center for Voting and Democracy

This nonprofit group is involved in voting systems reform and supports Instant Runoff Voting (IRV). The Web site includes frequently asked questions section about IRV and provides information and resources on the Voting Rights Act.

Constitution Project

The Constitution Project's Forum on Election Reform is a nonprofit organization of voter rights advocates, election officials, and policy experts that seeks bipartisan consensus on reform issues. The Forum's Web site provides information on current legislation and recent developments, as well as studies and its August 2001 report entitled "Building a Consensus on Election Reform."

Election Center

The Election Center is a nonprofit organization of government voting and election officials. It administers testing and certification of voting systems for the National Association of State Election Directors (NASED). The National Task Force on Election Reform released its report on July 9, 2001.

Electiononline.org

A joint project of the Pew Charitable Trusts and the University of Richmond. It is a clearinghouse for data, news, and analysis on election reform. The group published an election reform report and survey. In conjunction with the Constitution Project, it released a report on the provisional voting challenge on December 20, 2001.

League of Women Voters

The nonpartisan organization's Web site offers information on the League's position on and major recommendations for election administration reform.

The National Commission on Federal Election Reform (Carter/Ford Commission)
The Commission, organized by the Miller Center for Public Affairs and the Century Foundation, issued its report on July 31, 2001. The Commission's honorary co-chairmen are former Presidents Jimmy Carter and Gerald Ford.

114

Stateline.org

A joint project of the Pew Charitable Trust and the University of Richmond. It is operated by the Pew Center on the States, and the Web page features election reform issues with links to current state news on election reform actions, as well as a searchable database of election reform news.

This Calls for Reform

This Web site is sponsored by George Washington University. It offers a summary of electoral reform proposals since the 2000 election, including many state activities with links to the full text of some states' election reform reports.

---

[i] Document provided by the office of U.S. Senator Evan Bayh.

Appendix Two
House Consideration and Summary of H.R. 3295
(Ney-Hoyer bill) - Kevin Coleman [staff][i]

H.R. 3295, the "Help America Vote Act of 2002," was introduced on November 14, 2001 and referred to the following committees: House Administration, Judiciary, Science, Government Reform, and Armed Services. It was reported by the House Administration Committee and discharged by the Judiciary, Government Reform, and Armed Services Committees on December 10. The House took up the bill under a closed rule on December 12; the proposed rule for consideration was adopted on a 223-193 vote. The Ney-Hoyer bill was adopted by the House on December 12 on a 362-63 vote.

Rule for Consideration of Ney-Hoyer bill: H.Res. 311

Text of Ney – Manager's amendment: H. Rept. 107-331

House Administration Committee Report: H. Rept. 107-329

Summary of H.R. 3295

New Federal Agency
Election Assistance Commission (EAC)
Four members

- Four members appointed by President, (one each from list of nominees, submitted by Senate majority leader, Senate minority leader, Speaker of the House, and House minority leader)

- Establishes EAC Standards Board to review voluntary standards (110 members, state and local officials)
- Establishes EAC Board of Advisors to review voluntary standards (25 members, representatives of federal organizations, agencies, and national associations with election responsibilities)
- Authorizes funding for three fiscal years

Studies/reports required.

- Periodic studies available to public on election administration issues
- Recipients of grants for voting technologies research must file reports annually
- Inspectors general of the armed forces file annual reports on effectiveness of and compliance with voting assistance programs for overseas and armed forces voters

Specific study issues identified.

Current and alternate methods of:

- Ensuring accessibility to voting, registration, and polling places for disabled and voters with limited English proficiency
- Voting and vote-counting methods in federal elections
- Maintaining secure and accurate lists of voters (including establishment of statewide, centralized systems), and ensuring that all registered voters are on appropriate polling site lists
- Provisional voting

- Educating voters about registration and voting, using voting mechanisms, location of polling places
- Recruiting and improving performance of poll workers
- Ballot design
- Federal and state laws voter eligibility
- Election administration in urban and rural areas
- Registration for military and overseas voters, methods of ensuring timely delivery of ballots, and proper and expeditious handling and counting
- Conducting elections on different days, at different places, and during different hours, including advisability of establishing a uniform poll closing time
- Ways the federal government can best assist state and local officials to improve administration of federal elections and levels of funding needed

Minimum standards for voter registration, vote counting, second chance and provisional voting.

- Requirements that new voting systems give voters the opportunity to correct errors under conditions which assure privacy, except for replacements or upgrades within existing voting systems
- Requirements that new voting systems provide the means for voters with physical disabilities, including blindness, to cast a secret ballot
- States must provide for in-precinct provisional voting by 2002 elections, except in states where all votes are cast by mail
- Requires each state to establish an official statewide, networked voter registration system in states requiring registration
- Provisions to ensure accurate, updated registration records, including required removal of ineligible voters

- Uniform standards for what constitutes a vote for each certified voting system
- Safeguards for voting by uniformed and overseas voters

Standards enforcement.

- Standards implemented within two years of enactment
- Commission notifies Attorney General of states not in compliance and Attorney General may bring civil action

Voluntary standards for voting systems.

- Establishes a Technical Standards Development Committee to make recommendations for voluntary standards (members include Dir. Of National Institute of Standards and Technology, and 14 other members from Standards Board, Board of Advisors, Architectural and Transportation Barrier Compliance Board, the American National Standards Institute, and others with technical and scientific expertise)
- National Institute of Standards and Technology provides technical support in development of voluntary standards
- Develop, adopt, and update voluntary voting systems standards at least every four years
- Develop, adopt, and update voluntary standards for maintaining and enhancing accessibility and privacy of registration facilities, polling places, and voting methods, including for elderly and disabled at least every four years
- Develop, adopt, and update voluntary standards for federal election management practice for state and local officials at least every four years

Grant program funding.

- $400 million for punch card buyout and punch card enhancement programs (provides $6,000 per precinct to replace punch card voting systems where they were used in 2000 elections, or $2,000 per precinct to improve punch card voting systems; jurisdictions that receive funds for replacement will consider the use of new technology by voters with disabilities, including blindness)
- $2.25 billion for voting systems improvements program (election fund program for all states to improve voter registration, voting education, voting equipment, poll worker training, assure access for voters with disabilities, etc.)
- $20 million for research grants to improve voting technology (provides funding to entities engaged in research and development)
- $10 million for pilot program grants to test new voting technologies

Matching formula.

- 90% fed/10% state or local for punch card buyout and punch card improvement programs (95% fed for jurisdictions in lowest quartile median income nationally)
- 75% fed/25% state or local for voting systems improvement program (election fund)

Grant timetable/application process.

- For punch card buyout or enhancement programs, states submit application within 120 days of enactment (local governments may apply by Nov. 2002 election if state fails to submit application or is ineligible)
- States eligible for annual payment for voting systems improvements (election fund) if in compliance with requirements for program
- Research grants require submission of application to EAC
- Pilot program grants require submission of application to EAC

Grant program administered by

- Election Assistance Commission

Military voting provisions.

- Inspectors general of Army, Navy, Air Force, and Marine Corps conduct annual review of voting assistance programs and compliance with them
- Inspector general of DOD reports to Congress annually on voting assistance programs of the armed forces
- Requires that voter participation statistics be reported separately for military and for overseas voters
- Secretary of Defense certifies to Congress that a voting assistance officer has been appointed to perform voting assistance duties
- Secretary of each military department ensures members of military and dependents have access to registration and voting information
- Secretary of Defense will conduct periodic surveys of mail shipments during the four months preceding an election, and will ensure that a postmark or proof of mailing date is provided on each absentee ballot

- Requires each state to designate a single office to provide information concerning absentee registration and voting in the state
- States required to accept post card forms as a simultaneous voter registration and absentee ballot application for all federal elections in the state for the next two federal election cycles
- States required to use a standard oath prescribed by presidential designee if oath or affirmation is required

Poll worker recruiting programs.

- Establishes the "Help America Vote Program" to encourage college students to serve as nonpartisan poll workers and to encourage state and local governments to use students in that capacity; grants provided for projects and activities; authorizes $5 million for FY 2002 and necessary sums for future years
- Establishes a federally chartered corporation known as the "Help America Vote Foundation" to recruit high school students to participate as nonpartisan poll workers. Authorizes $5 million for FY 2002.

---

[i] Document provided by the office of U.S. Congressman Mark Souder.

Appendix Three

Voting System Vendors[i]

EDS (http://www.eds.com) - online secure voting for the military (in cooperation with Identix)

Election.com (http:///www.election.com/us/index.htm) - complete election management systems - voter registration and database management, pollsite and remote electronic

Election Systems & Software (http:///www.essvote.com) - hardware, software and services for all phases of the election/voting cycle; ADA accessible electronic voting system

Glogal Election Software (http://www.gesn.com) - Accuvote TS System - ADA accessible

Hart Intercivic (http://www.hartintercivic.com) - direct record electronic voting systems; ADA accessible

Identix (http:///www.indentix.com)- Internet registration, absentee ballot application, and voting for overseas military personnel (in cooperation with EDS)

QuadMedia (http://www.kioskinfo.com)- electronic touch screen voting systems; ADA accessible

Sequoia Pacific (http://www.seqpac.com)- election supplies and services; AVC Advantage System - ADA accessible

VoteHere (http://www.votehere.net)- electronic systems for polling places and remote Internet voting

Voting Technologies International (http://www.vtintl.com)

---

[i] This list of voting system vendors from the National Conference of State Legislatures is available online at http://www.ncsl.org/programs/legman/elect/taskfc/vendors.htm

Selected Bibliography

Albright, Spencer D. 1942. *The American Ballot*. Washington, DC: American Council on Public Affairs.

Almond, Gabriel A. and Sydney Verba. 1963. *The Civic Culture*. Boston, MA: Little, Brown.

Aristotle. 322 B.C. *"A Treatise on Government."* Translated from the Greek by William Ellis. Available online at: http://www.literaturepage.com/read/treatiseongovernment.html

Arnold, R. Douglas. 1990. *The Logic of Congressional Action*. New Haven, CT: Yale University.

Babbie, Earl R. 2001. *The Practice of Social Research*. 10th ed. London, UK: Wadsworth/Thomson Learning.

Beilenson, Peter and Helen Beilenson. 1982. *The Wit and Wisdom of Franklin D. Roosevelt, Government and Democracy*. White Plains, NY: Peter Pauper Press.

Brady, Henry E., Justin Buchler, Matt Jarvis, and John McNulty. 2001. "Counting All The Votes: The Performance of Voting Technology in the United States." Available online at: http://ucdata.berkeley.edu/new_web/countingallthevotes.pdf.

Caltech/MIT Voting Technology Project. March 2001. "Residual Votes Attributable to Technology." Available online at: http://www.hss.caltech.edu/%7Evoting/CalTech_MIT_Report_Version2.pdf.

Caltech/MIT Voting Technology Project. July 2001. "Voting: What Is, What Could Be." Available online at: www.vote.caltech.edu/Reports/index.html.

Cigler, Allen J. and Burdett A. Loomis. 2002. *Interest Group Politics*. Washington, DC: CQ Press.

Dahl, Robert. 1956. *A Preface to Democratic Theory*. Chicago, IL: University of Chicago Press.

Dahl, Robert. 1961. *Who Governs? Democracy and Power in an American City.* New Haven, CT: Yale University Press.

Davidson, Roger H. 1969. The *Role of the Congressman.* New York, NY: Pegasus.

De La Garza, Rudolfo O., Louis DeSipio, F. Chris Garcia, John Garcia, and Angelo Falcon. 1992. *Latino Voices.* Boulder, CO: Westview Press.

Delli Carpini, Michael X. and Scott Keeter. 1996. *What Americans Know About Politics and Why It Matters.* New Haven, CT: Yale University Press.

Dudley, Robert L. and Alan R. Gitelson. 2002. *American Elections: The Rules Matter.* New York, NY: Longman.

Elazar, Daniel J. 1994. *The American Mosaic: The Impact of Space, Time, and Culture on American Politics.* Boulder, CO: Westview Press.

Epstein, Richard A. 2001. "In Such Manner as the Legislature Thereof May Direct: The Outcome in *Bush v. Gore* Defended." In Cass R. Sunstein and Richard A. Epstein (eds) *The Vote: Bush, Gore & The Supreme Court.* Chicago, IL: University of Chicago Press.

"Election Reform Briefing: Ready for Reform," *electionline.org* and The Constitution Project election reform initiative, March 2003 available online at: http://www.electionline.org/site/dav/pdf/eripbrief32003.pdf.

Federal Election Commission. 2002b. "About Elections and Voting." Available online at: www.fec.gov/pages/dre.htm.

Fife, Brian and Geralyn M. Miller. 2002. *Political Culture in the United States.* Westport, CT: Greenwood Publishing.

Fopay, Dave. 2003. "County to Discuss Dropping Number of Polling Places." *Journal Gazette & Times-Courier.* June 26.

Frost, Robert. 1915. *North of Boston.* New York, NY: Henry Holt & Company.

Gibson, Rachel. 2001/2002. "Elections Online: Assessing Internet Voting in Light of the Arizona Democratic Primary." *Political Science Quarterly.* 116(4):561-584.

Graber, Doris. 1993. Processing the News: How People Tame the Information Tide. Lanham, MD: University Press of America.

Grodzins, Mortin. 1966. *The American System.* Chicago, IL: Rand-McNally.

Grossman, Harvey. October 26, 2002. "Punch-card voting system must be retired." Voice of the People Letter, *Chicago Tribune.*

Hedge, David M. and Michael J. Scicchitano. 1994. "Regulating in Space and Time: The Case of Regulatory Federalism." *Journal of Politics.* 56(1):134-153.

Institute of Government and Public Affairs. 2002. *The Machinery of Democracy: Voting Systems and Ballot Miscounts in Illinois.* Available online at: http://www.igpa.uiuc.edu/publications/critIssues/default.htm#democracy.

Jewell, Malcolm. 2001. *Political Parties and Elections in American States.* Washington, DC: CQ Press.

Kingdon, John W. 1995. *Agendas, Alternatives, and Public Policies.* 2nd ed. New York, NY: HarperCollins.

Kingdon, John W. 1989. *Congressmen's Voting Decisions,* 3rd ed. New York, NY: Harper & Row.

Knack, Stephen. 1995. "Does 'Motor Voter' Work? Evidence from State-Level Data." *Journal of Politics.* 57(3):796-811.

Knack, Stephen and Martha Kropf. 2002. "Who Used Inferior Voting Technology?" *PS: Political Science and Politics.* 35(3):541-8.

Kropf, Martha. 2003. "Soft Money and Issue Advocacy in the 2002 Missouri Senate Election." Paper presented at the Midwest Political Science Association.

Kuhn, Thomas. 1996. *The Structure of Scientific Revolutions.* Chicago, IL: University of Chicago Press.

Lasswell, Harold Dwight. 1958. *Politics: Who Gets What, When, How.* New York, NY: Meridian Books.

Lindblom, Charles E. 1995. "The Science of Muddling Through." In Stella Z. Theodoulou and Matthew A. Cahn (eds): *Public Policy: The Essential Readings.* Englewood Cliffs, NJ: Prentice Hall.

Lindblom, Charles E. 1959. "The Science of Muddling Through." *American Public Administration Review.* 19:79-88.

Lipsky, Michael. 1980. *Street-Level Bureaucracy: Dilemmas of the Individual in Public Service.* New York, NY: Russell Sage Foundation.

Majone, Giandomenico and Aaron B. Wildavsky. 1995. "Implementation as Evolution." In Stella Z. Theodoulou and Matthew A. Cahn (eds): *Public Policy: The Essential Readings.* Englewood Cliffs, NJ: Prentice Hall.

Martel, Leon. 1986. *Mastering Change.* New York, NY: New American Library.

Mayfield, Loomis. 1993. "Voting Fraud in Early Twentieth-Century Pittsburgh." *Journal of Interdisciplinary History.* 29(1):59-84.

Mayhew, David R. 1974. *Congress: The Electoral Connection.* New Haven, CT: Yale University Press.

Moore, George H. 1884. "Notes on Tithing-Men and the Ballot." *Proceedings of the American Antiquarian Society.* Worcester, MA: Press of Chas. Hamilton.

Neale, Gregory B. 1994. *Organizational Behavior: A Management Challenge.* Fort Worth, TX: Dryden Press.

Olson, Mancur. 1971. *The Logic of Collective Action.* Cambridge, MA: Harvard University Press.

Page, Benjamin I. and Robert Y. Shapiro. 1992. *The Rational Public.* Chicago, IL: University of Chicago Press.

Popper, Karl. 1959/1992. *The Logic of Scientific Discovery.* New York, NY: Routledge, Inc.

Pressman, Jeffrey L. and Aaron B. Wildavsky. 1973. *Implementation.* Berkeley, CA: University of California Press.

Rosenthal, Alan. 1993. *The Third House: Lobbyists and Lobbying in the States.* Washington, DC: Congressional Quarterly Press.

Rhine, Staci L. 1996. "An Analysis of the Impact of Registration Factors on Turnout in 1992." *Political Behavior.* 18(2):171-185.

Schattschneider, Elmer E. 1975. *The Semi-Sovereign People.* Hinsdale, IL: Dryden Press.

Schlozman, Kay Lehman and John T. Tierney. 1986. *Organized Interests and American Democracy.* New York, NY: Harper & Row.

Smith, Steven S. and Christopher J. Deering. 1984. *Committees in Congress.* Washington, DC: CQ Press.

Sorauf, Frank. 1957. "The Public Interest Reconsidered." *Journal of Politics.* 19:619-635.

Thomas, Robert D. 1979. "Implementing Federal Programs." *Political Science Quarterly.* 94(3):419-435.

Uhlmann, Michael M. 2001. "Federalism and Election Reform." *Texas Review of Law and Politics.* 6:491-512.

Walker, Jack L. Jr. 1983. "The Origins and Maintenance of Interest Groups in America." *American Political Science Review.* 77:390-406.

Walker, Jack L., Jr. 1991. *Mobilizing Interest Groups in America.* Ann Arbor, MI: University of Michigan Press.

"A Modern Democracy That Can't Count Votes." Editorial, *Los Angeles Times*, December 11, 2000.

Wilson, Woodrow. 1887. "The Science of Administration." *Political Science Quarterly* 2(2):197-222.

Zukerman, T. David. 1927. "The Voting Machine Extends Its Territory." *American Political Science Review.* 21(3):603-610; p. 609.

Legal Cases

Black v. McGuffage, No. 01-01C208 No. 01 C796, 209 F. Supp 2d 889 (March 29, 2002).

Bush v. Gore, 531 U.S. 98 (December 9, 2000).

Index

African-American 27, 45-46, 53, 66

Albright, Spencer D. 5-6, 11

Almond, Gabriel A. 98

American Association of People With Disabilities 46, 57

American Enterprise Institute 53

American Public Administration Review 89

Americans With Disabilities Act 46, 72, 80, 94

Ansolabehere, Stephen 66, 77

Aristotle 79

Arnold, R. Douglas 49, 54, 60

Association of Trial Lawyers of America 50-51

Babbie, Earl R. 30

Berry, Jeffrey M. 57

Berry, Mary Frances Berry 43, 52, 57

Bipartisan 15, 41-42, 61, 77

Black v. McGuffage 45, 57, 70

Blackwell, Kenneth 48, 57

Brady, Henry E. 33

Buchler, Justin 33

Bush, U.S. President George i, 3, 66

Bush v. Gore 24, 33, 54, 75, 81

Caltech 18-21, 23, 26, 33, 42, 66

Carter, U.S. President Jimmy 41

Chicago Tribune 18-19, 32, 97

Cigler Allen J. 8

Civil rights 19, 43, 25

Civil Rights Act 43

Coleridge, Samuel Taylor 59

Coles County, Illinois 71

Culture (culturally) 21-22, 83, 91, 101, notes

Cumulative voting 97 notes

Dahl, Robert 1, 8, 93, 96

Davidson, Roger H. 71

Deering, Christopher J. 37

De La Garza, Rudolfo 44

Delli, Carpini, Michael X. 98

Dickson, James C. 57

Democracy 1-3, 4, 7, 9, 14, 42, 52, 55, 92-102

Democrat 41, 53

Democratic 4, 9, 14-15, 42, 44, 55, 93, 98-100

Direct record electronic voting equipment (DRE) 4, 6, 15, 19, 49, 83, 89

Di Sippio, Louis 44

Dickson, James C. 46 notes

Dodd, U.S. Congressman Christopher 41, 57

Dudley, Robert L. 7

Elazar, Daniel J. 22

Election Assistance Committee 61, 77, 80

Election Center, The 48, 57

Election 2000 2-3, 17-18, 21, 24, 27, 29, 36, 38, 42-43, 50, 52-54, 59-61, 65-66, 68, 73-74, 83, 88

Electoral College i, 23, 38

Epstein, Richard A. 54

Equal protection 15, 20, 43, 52, 55, 69, 77, 79, 81, 82, 84, 94-95

Falcon, Angelo 44

Federal Election Commission (FEC) 50, 56, 83, notes

Federal Election Campaign Act 75

Fife, Brian L. 6, 21, 84, notes

Fopay, Dave 71

Ford, U.S. President Gerald 41

Frost, Robert 1, 15

Garcia, F. Chris 44

Garcia, John 44

Gibson, Rachel 84

Gitelson, Alan R. 7

Graber, Doris 30

Grodzins, Mortin 13

Grossman, Harvey 32

Hastert, U.S. House Speaker Dennis 59 notes

Hedge, David M. 80

Help America Vote Act (HAVA) i-ii, 3, 9, 12, 15, 37-39, 50, 55, 59-63, 67-68, 70-77, 79-82, 84-86, 88-89, 91-92, 94-95, 98-100

Help America Vote Foundation 100

Hispanic-American 44-46, 66

Ideology(ies) 7-9, 31, 36, 53

Incremental(ism) ii, 12, 14, 29, 76-77, 89-90, 92, 99

Interest group 13-14, 24, 59, 66, 68, 72, 76, 88, 95

I-voting 84-85

Jarvis, Matt 33

Jewell, Malcolm 22

Johnson, U.S. President Lyndon 79

Jurisdiction(s) 2, 11, 19, 24-26, 68, 73, 80, 82-85, 91

Keeter, Scott 98

Kingdon, John 32, 61

Knack, Stephen 26-27, 77

Kropf, Martha 25, 69

Kuhn, Thomas 30

Laswell, Harold 33

Lawyers Committee for Civil Rights Under the Law 69, 77

Lehman, Kay 9

Lewis, Doug 48, 57

Lindblom, Charles E. 12, 89-90

Lippmann, Walter 35, 57

Lipsky, Michael 86-87

Loomis, Burdett A. 8, 11

Lott, John 53, 57

Machiavelli 17

Majone, Giandomenico 86-87

Martel, Leon 10

Mayfield, Loomis 11

Mayhew, David R. 42

McNulty, John 33

Mechanical lever machine 5, 11, 15, 18

Media 2, 4, 6, 17, 24, 27-29, 38, 43, 97

Medill, Joseph 97

Mercuri, Rebecca 83

Mfume, Kweisi 43, 45, 57

Miami Herald 27, 50, 57

Military 39, 74

Miller, Geralyn M. i-ii, 6, 21, 41, 84

MIT 7, 8, 18-21, 23, 25, 33, 42, 66

Moore, George H. 495

Motor Voter Act 9

National Association for the Advancement of Colored People (NAACP) 43-45, 57

National Commission on Federal

National Council of LaRaza 45, 57

National Science Foundation 85

National Voter Registration Act 73

Neale, Gregory B. 42

O'Dell, Walden 50

Olson, Mancur 7

Operating budget 21, 48, 69

Optical scan voting equipment 15, 18, 25

Orr, Cook County, Illinois Clerk David 4, 15

Page, Benjamin I. 32

Paper ballot 4-5, 15, 18

Parker, Laura 33

Pew Charitable Trust 70

Phillips, Deborah M. 48, 57, 74

Polyarchal 93

Popper, Karl 28-29, 77, 90, 99-100

Pressman, Jeffrey L. 86

Puerto Rican Legal Defense and Education Fund 72

Punch card voting equipment i-ii, 5-6, 15, 17-18, 19, 21, 25-26, 32, 61, 64, 66-68, 71, 81-82, notes

Registered voters 5, 6, 73, 83

Republican 41, 50

Republican National Committee (RNC) 50

Rhine, Staci L. 27

Roosevelt, U.S. President Franklin Delano 77, 93

Rosenthal, Alan 8

Sabato 42, 57, 67, 77

Schattschneider, Elmer E. 14

Schlozman, Kay 8

Scicchitano, Michael J. 80

Self-government (governance) 2, 13, 15, 31, 95-96, 98

Self-interest 3, 36, 43, 55, 90, 95

Shapiro, Robert Y. 32

Smith, Richard A. 51, 57

Smith, Steven S. 37

Sorauf, Frank 31-32

Tennyson, Alfred Lord 77

Texas Law Review 68

Thernstrom, Abigail 52-53, 57

Thomas, Robert D. 80

Tierney, John T. 8

Turnout 1-2, 27, 84

Uhlmann, Michael M. 57

U.S. Commission on Civil Rights 33, 43, 52, 57

U.S. House Committee on Science 77

U.S. House Judiciary Committee 23-24, 57, 67

U.S. House Committee on Rules and Administration 57

U.S. Senate Committee on Rules and Administration 77

U.S. Supreme Court 75, 81

Unintended consequences 14, 29, 31, 77, 89-90, 96-98, 100

United Cerebral Palsy Association 47, 57, 72

Verba 98

Voting equipment / technology i-ii, 4-6, 9, 11, 17-21, 24-26, 33, 38, 40, 42, 45-47, 49-50, 64-72, 76, 81-84, 86, 89, 101

Voting Integrity Project, The 48-49, 57, 74, 77

Voting Rights Act 9, 72

Voting Rights Language Assistance Act 72

Walker, Jack L. 8

Wheeler, Charles 77, 98

Wildavsky, Aaron B. 86-87

Wilson, Woodrow 33

Williams, Robert 46-47, 57

Witness 8, 24, 37, 39, 42-43, 50, 67, 74, 87

Yzabuirre, Raul 45, 57

Zuckerman, T. David 12, 15, 132

STUDIES IN POLITICAL SCIENCE

1. David R. Jones, **Political Parties and Policy Gridlock in American Government**
2. Jong-Sup Lee and Uk Heo, **The U.S.-South Korean Alliance, 1961-1988: Free-Riding or Bargaining?**
3. Rachel K. Gibson, **The Growth of Anti-Immigrant Parties in Western Europe**
4. Derek S. Reveron, **Promoting Democracy in the Post-Soviet Region**
5. James R. Hedtke, **Lame Duck Presidents–Myth or Reality**
6. Gerson Moreno-Riaño, **Political Tolerance, Culture, and the Individual**
7. Rosa Gomez Dierks, **Credible Fiscal Policy Commitments and Market Access–Case Studies of Argentina, Chile, and Mexico, 1980-1995**
8. James Biser Whisker, **The Supremacy of the State in International Law: The Act of State Doctrine**
9. Henry Flores, **The Evolution of the Liberal Democratic State with a Case Study of Latinos in San Antonio, Texas**
10. Joseph L. Wert, **A Study of Bill Clinton's Presidential Approval Ratings**
11. Philip Benwell, **In Defence of Australia's Constitutional Monarchy**
12. Janet Campbell, **An Analysis of Law in the Marxist Tradition**
13. Michael J. Zarkin, **Social Learning and the History of U.S. Telecommunications Policy, 1900-1996: Creating the Telecommunications Act of 1996**
14. Herbert P. LePore, **The Politics and Failure of Naval Disarmament, 1919-1939: The Phantom Peace**
15. Matthew T. Kenney, **A Theoretical Examination of Political Values and Attitudes in New and Old Democracies**
16. John Randolph LeBlanc, **Ethics and Creativity in the Political Thought of Simone Weil and AlbertCamus**
17. Terri Jett, **Agenda-Setting and Decision-Making of African American County Officials: The Case of Wilcox County**
18. Bruce A. Carroll, **The Role, Design, and Growing Importance of United States Magistrate Judges**
19. Youngtae Shin, **Women and Politics in Japan and Korea**
20. Geralyn M. Miller, **Changing the Way America Votes–Election Reform, Incrementalism, and Cutting Deals**